ELKRIDGE

PATH

Double Your Net Worth

And Passive Income Every Year

PATRICK ROGERS

ROBERT INDRIES

Edited and Published With The Help Of

Fernando Labastida

Book Cover Art and Illustrations by Robert Indries

2026

PRAISE FOR ELKRIDGE PATH

“Elkridge path clearly outlines every single step towards acquiring tens of millions in net worth during your career. If you invest within the US, this is a must read.”

Aaron Scott Young
CEO of Laughlin Associates (250K+ US Companies Incorporated)

“Forget following the pack. I've always carved my own path, and Elkridge Path is clearly for those carving their own fast-track to wealth in a way that just makes sense.”

Tracy Hazzard
CEO of Podetize (500+ Podcasts Hosted)

"After three decades of building businesses, I’ve figured a few things out. However, I’ve never found a single source of knowledge that captures all of the things I needed to learn like Elkridge Path does. It’s the perfect guidebook for doubling your net worth, over and over again."

Brian Massey
$1B+ In Online Sales Generated

"I love what Robert has done with HOW Sessions and strongly recommend everyone to try it. I'm doing one myself this week on a particular issue I'm working on!"

Patrick Grove
Forbes Richest, Took 6 Companies From Startup To IPO

"A practical roadmap for creating generational wealth through thoughtful acquisitions, disciplined growth, and strategic exits."

Dr. Greg S. Reid
Founder of Secret Knock, Award-Winning Author & Film Producer

"As both a founder and investor, I've seen firsthand that real wealth isn't built from hustle alone—it's built from clarity, ownership, and intentional systems. Elkridge Path captures that shift beautifully."

Laurel Mintz
Award-Winning Investor, VC Fund Manager, Grew 400+ Brands

Their roadmap mirrors what I have seen across closing billions in partnership-driven growth. When strategy, people, and capital are properly aligned, wealth stops being linear and becomes exponential. This book gives readers that alignment blueprint."

Kyle Kane
Inc. 500 Fastest Growing, TEDx Speaker, Emmy Winner

CONTENTS

DISCLAIMER

This book contains information the authors believe to be accurate, at the time of its writing and on the subject matters it covers, but it is sold with the understanding that neither the authors nor the publisher is offering individualized advice tailored to any specific portfolio or to any individual's particular needs, or rendering investment advice or other professional services such as legal or accounting advice. A competent professional's services should be sought if one needs expert assistance in areas that include investment, legal, and accounting advice.

This book references performance data collected over several years. Past results do not guarantee future performance.

More so, the performance of various portfolios and the laws and regulations that govern their operation change over time, which could change the status of the information in this book. This book solely provides historical data to discuss and illustrate the underlying principles. Additionally, this book is not intended to serve as the basis for any financial decision.

No warranty is made with respect to the accuracy or completeness of the information contained herein, and both the authors and the publisher specifically disclaim any responsibility for any liability, loss, or risk, personal or otherwise, which is incurred as a consequence, directly or indirectly, of the use and application of any of the contents of this book.

Finally, in the text that follows, some people's names and identifying characteristics have been changed.

ABOUT THE AUTHORS

Patrick Rogers is a US Naval Officer Veteran who used his military-grade determination, discipline, and patience to build profitable asset portfolios, both for himself and for his clients. With well over $250 million in small business transactions, Patrick is one of the M&A leaders in the US. He's also leading the way towards bringing wealth acquisition strategies and services, available before just to the ultra-rich, to those of us who are not quite there, yet.

Robert Indries was born into a modest family in a small Romanian town. Since then, he's built several profitable businesses in the US and Europe, generating millions in revenue every year and over $500 million for his clients. While building his little empire, Robert has traveled to or lived in a dozen different countries, pulling in hundreds of different perspectives and insights into his wealth creation strategies. Robert's focus is on building business systems that scale.

ACKNOWLEDGEMENTS

This book is dedicated to all of the amazing individuals we've had and continue to have the privilege of learning from. We mention a few of them in this book, and we gladly reference their books.

Many people have said that the main driver of our evolution, as individuals, are the people we meet and the books we read. And we couldn't agree more. We've learned from late authors such as Napoleon Hill, contemporary billionaires such as Patrick Grove, and everyone in between.

We've learned from our parents, our teachers, our friends, our partners, and our children. Oh... how much we've learned from our children...

Our work for Elkridge Path was not to invent anything. Instead, it was the selection of the absolute most critical principles and strategies that double a person's net worth and passive income in the shortest possible time.

This book is testament to the results we can attain by learning from and working with others. And we're taking this moment just to thank everyone that's been with us on this journey.

FOREWORD

I met Robert years ago. I was looking for a team that can generate a consistent flow of qualified leads for my healthcare clinic.

From the very first month, his team was able to deliver high quality booked appointments, in what I knew to be a difficult niche.

I actually haven't spoken to Robert at all during the first month or so of my engagement with his marketing firm. His team just felt that we're quite similar, and suggested we meet one to one.

To this day I think about that... Their marketing team attracted me as a client. Their sales team closed the deal. Their delivery team was generating leads for my business. Their customer success team was keeping us updated every week. Everything was going well. Yet, I haven't seen or heard from the owner, not even once...

Now that's a real business. One that's 100% self-sufficient.

I've heard about the concept before. I've read about it in books. But I've never actually seen it in practice. At least not at this level.

Robert could have easily been on a 6-mo vacation, earning passive income from this cashflowing asset I was working with.

Once I started speaking with him, it was clear his team was spot on. We resonated beautifully on topics of values, faith, interests, and business. So we stayed in touch, speaking on calls from time to time.

During that period, I was trying to make my own company self-sufficient. I was at my second COO, and it wasn't going as well as I had hoped.

Months later, on one of our calls, Robert said "why don't you just rent out my administrative team?"

Long story short, they came in and, one by one, they started helping with every part of operations... Customer relations, service delivery, finances, IT, anything I basically needed done, their team could get done.

I could finally step away from the day to day of my company and look at other opportunities I had in front of me.

This allowed me to not just acquire a second clinic, but also eventually accept the role of Global Medical Director at Amazon. A full-time role that I had the privilege of being invited for, that I wouldn't have been able to take, if it wasn't for Elkridge's business management team helping run day to day ops in my clinics.

It's not even been two full years and I've already added more than 7-figures to my net worth. Seeing everything with my own eyes makes me realize how much faster we can all reach our goals.

I'm not saying it's easy, or that it's not scary sometimes, but it's definitely worth it.

To anyone reading this book: You're in the right place. Best of luck on your journey, and let Elkridge's principles guide you on this path.

Anthony N. Harris

Global Medical Director, Amazon

INTRODUCTION

WHY THIS BOOK EXISTS

Most people spend their entire lives working but never learning how wealth actually works. Even those that have reached high levels of success in their careers or with their companies, in their 50s or later, look at a few hundred grand (or maybe 7-figures, if they're lucky) in their bank account, and are left wondering: Is that it?

And those with 6-7 figures saved are the lucky ones. Too many don't even reach that level.

We wrote *Elkridge Path* to change that. To show everyone a clear path to 8- and 9-figure empires, effectively recession-proofing our lives, for as long as we'll live.

Over the past two decades, we've built, bought, and scaled companies across multiple industries. We've advised entrepreneurs, executives, and investors who started from nothing and went on to create multi-million-dollar portfolios and lasting freedom. Along the way, we discovered that true wealth follows predictable patterns. When you understand those patterns—and apply them with discipline—you can double your net worth and passive income every year.

That's not hype. It's a process. It's math. It's what we've done, and what we now help others do.

We wrote this book because most financial advice focuses on just one stage—getting out of debt, or investing, or exiting a business—without showing how it all connects. But wealth isn't one event. It's a progression, a system you build step by step.

Elkridge Path gives you that system.

It's a roadmap tested by real business owners, investors, and ambitious professionals who've walked this path before you—and proven it works.

Whether you're just starting to get ahead, already own a business, or are preparing to create a legacy that lasts for generations, this book meets you where you are and gives you the exact tools to move forward faster.

This is the guide we wish we'd had twenty years ago.

THE THREE-PART JOURNEY

This book is divided into three parts—each one meeting you exactly where you are on your wealth journey.

We've learned through experience that the skills, mindset, and systems required to go from zero to $300,000 are slightly different from those needed to turn $300,000 into millions, and then later on, those required to turn millions into generational wealth.

Each stage has its own rules, challenges, and rewards. Master each one, and you'll compound wealth at an exponential rate.

PART I: IMPROVE YOUR BALANCE SHEET

Part I distills the top ten principles—out of hundreds of principles—that consistently help people reach $300,000 in investable assets.

We designed this section for those who are just getting started: maybe you have a job, maybe you run a small business, but you don't yet have the capital to acquire larger assets or invest at scale.

This section focuses on the fundamentals that move the needle fastest: How to expand income without working more hours. How to systematize savings so wealth builds automatically. How to develop the mindset that creates opportunity instead of scarcity. How to organize your personal finances like a small business

The goal of Part I is simple: help you reach that first milestone—$300,000 in investable assets.

That number isn't arbitrary. It's the threshold where you gain access to the next level of opportunities—where you can start acquiring, automating, and compounding real wealth.

We've applied these principles ourselves and seen others go from living paycheck to paycheck to crossing that mark in a few short years.

If you're still in that building phase, Part I is where your journey begins.

PART II: TURN ASSETS INTO PASSIVE INCOME

Once you've built your foundation, it's time to turn cash into significant levels of passive income. That's where **Part II** comes in.

This section is designed for people who have already reached that $300,000 mark—through their corporate career and/or through building an established business.

We show you how to acquire truly healthy, cash-flowing assets, structure deals intelligently, and automate operations so your assets keep generating passive income with minimal owner dependency.

This is where you stop trading time for money. This is where we turn 6-figures into millions. This is where the fun starts.

PART III: CREATE GENERATIONAL WEALTH

By the time you reach Part III, you're already operating at a high level. You've acquired assets, automated cash flow, and built systems that compound value. Now, the goal shifts from personal wealth to *generational* wealth.

Here, we teach you how to scale from a successful investor to an empire builder.

You'll learn how to: combine multiple businesses into roll-ups that command higher valuations. Plan and time your exits strategically to maximize returns. Protect and preserve your wealth for future generations. Design a legacy that transcends money—through stewardship, mentorship, and giving back.

Part III is where you move from playing the wealth game to owning it. It's about multiplying your impact while creating the kind of freedom most people only dream about.

Together, these three parts form a complete roadmap—a proven path from financial survival to generational significance. The habits you'll form in Part I will make you sharper in Part II, and the systems you master in Part II will make you unstoppable in Part III.

WHY WE WROTE THIS BOOK THIS WAY

Some readers will start at the very beginning, learning how to build capital from scratch. Others already own some assets and are ready to start investing. A few may be reading this with millions in assets, searching for the strategy that can take them to the next level.

You don't need to read this book front to back. Each part is self-contained and immediately actionable. You can start wherever you are financially, and come back to earlier or later parts as you grow.

We built *Elkridge Path* as a tool, not a textbook. Every idea has been field-tested with real business owners, investors, and high-net-worth families. The language is simple on purpose.

Because wealth creation is cyclical, you'll revisit these same principles at higher levels as you grow. The discipline that helps you manage your first $10,000 feeds the disciplines that help you scale to $10 million. *Elkridge Path* gives you a framework that compounds alongside your wealth.

That's why we didn't fill these pages with theory or motivational fluff. You'll find action steps, examples, and strategies that produce measurable results.

Our goal is to make the process of building wealth *predictable*, *repeatable*, and *purpose-driven*, whether you're growing your first savings account or orchestrating a multi-company roll-up.

A QUICK NOTE ON WRITING STYLE

We, Patrick and Robert, have co-written and co-edited the entire book, and agree on all the points presented. As such, we've decided to express ourselves as co-narrators throughout the entire book. This means that even when either of us have a personal story to share, that story will be told from our joint voice, going from "I once had a situation where..." to "Patrick once had a situation where..." or "I then felt..." to "Robert then felt..."

This way, the entire book follows the same style, with two co-narrators sharing every story and every lesson, making it simpler to follow throughout.

THE PROMISE OF THE PATH

Wealth isn't just about money. It's about options.

It's about having the freedom to decide how you spend your time, who you work with, and what legacy you leave behind. It's the ability to live by design, not by default.

Elkridge Path exists to give you that freedom—step by step.

When we say you can "double your net worth and passive income every year," it's not a marketing slogan. It's a goal we've seen our clients achieve, again and again, by following this framework. They do it not through luck, or risky bets, but through disciplined strategy, focused execution, and the compounding effect of smart decisions made consistently over time.

That's the real promise of this book: You'll learn a process that transforms effort into very significant amounts of wealth. You'll learn how to create leverage without burnout, how to grow without chaos, and how to build prosperity that outlives you. We've watched this transformation happen hundreds of times. The moment someone understands that wealth can be engineered, they never go back.

That's what we want for you.

Whether your dream is to buy your first business, fund your children's future, give more generously, or simply never worry about bills or the economy, ever again, *Elkridge Path* gives you that roadmap.

PART 1

IMPROVE YOUR BALANCE SHEET

"Incredible change happens in your life when you decide to take control of what you have power over instead of craving control over what you don't."
— Steve Maraboli

CHAPTER 1

YOUR PERSONAL BALANCE SHEET

Here's a sobering statistic: 99.9% of people never reach $1 million in net worth.

Think about that for a moment. Nearly everyone you've ever known—your neighbors, your coworkers, your friends—will never experience true financial abundance. The kind of abundance where you don't *need* to work, but you work because you *want* to.

Why?

The main reason isn't lack of intelligence. It's not a lack of opportunity. It's a lack of financial literacy.

And here's the uncomfortable truth: most people don't want to admit they're not financially literate. They don't want to feel dumb. Many avoid learning about money altogether...

But here's what we need you to understand: you never actually "learn" financial literacy the way you learn history or math in school. It's a skill you develop by doing—by tracking your numbers, making decisions, and experiencing the outcomes of those decisions firsthand.

This chapter is going to change that for you.

Whether you're starting from zero or you already have some money in the bank, there's something here that will level up your life.

But where exactly are you starting from? Most people go through this world without ever knowing their actual financial position. Yes, they have a vague sense of what they make, what they owe, and what they're worth. But vague doesn't build wealth. Clarity does.

Here's a question we ask people all the time: Can you tell us your exact net worth right now? Not an estimate or a ballpark figure. The actual number?

If you can't answer that question within a few hundred dollars, you're (almost) flying blind. And it's much harder to navigate your way to financial freedom if you don't know where you are.

WHAT YOU FOCUS ON GROWS

Before we dive into the mechanics, let's talk about why this matters.

There's a principle–attributed to Thomas Monson–that applies to every area of life:

"When performance is measured, performance improves. When performance is measured and reported, the rate of improvement accelerates."

If you want to lose weight, you weigh yourself regularly. If you want to build muscle, you track your lifts. If you want to grow your business, you monitor your key metrics.

Anything that's important to you, you should track and measure. The parts of life you give energy to grow. The parts you neglect tend to deplete.

Your health? If you don't actively focus on it, it declines. Your relationships? They whither away.

And guess what? This same principle applies to wealth.

The simple act of regularly measuring your financial position tends to improve the rate at which it grows. We've seen this happen hundreds of times. Someone creates their first balance sheet, starts updating it regularly, and within a year their net worth has increased faster than ever before.

Why? Because you can't improve what you don't measure. And once you start measuring something, your brain naturally looks for ways to improve that number.

As Manson said: "When performance is measured, performance improves."

This has been proven time and time again in almost every business. The moment you start measuring something, performance in that area starts to improve, almost automatically.

If you want to improve your odds of becoming wealthy as quickly as possible, you need to measure your progress. And the more often you measure it, the better.

DOWN TO THE LAST $100

When Robert was in his late teens and early twenties, he consumed every self-help book and audio program he could find. Brian Tracy, Tony Robbins, Robin Sharma. This was before audiobooks existed—we're talking CD audio programs he'd listen to every day.

He absorbed all this inspirational content, and made a decision that seemed right at the time: he would give the world as much value as he could, and would ask others to pay him based on what they considered his efforts were worth.

So Robert started doing business that way.

When he completed work for clients, he would ask them: "How much do you think it's worth?"

Robert thought he was being generous. Humble. Service-oriented.

It was a horrible business strategy... absolutely horrible.

Robert had $50,000 saved up when he started his first business. But he lost Every. Single. Dollar. He was struggling like crazy, barely surviving.

About 3 years in, Robert looked at his bank account:

$100.

That's all he had left.

Robert sat down and did the math. At the time, he could buy a Subway sandwich for about $3. If he ate one sandwich per day and nothing else, he could survive for exactly one month.

So that's what he did. One sandwich. Three dollars. Every single day.

He lost a lot of weight during that time. He was incredibly thin. He developed a perfect six-pack—completely unintentional, obviously. There's nothing glamorous about starving...

But that wasn't the worst part.

During the first few days of living on $3 a day, Robert got a phone call from Europe. (he was living in Mexico at the time)

It was his aunt—his mother's sister. Robert's mother couldn't call him herself because she was in a dark place.

Grandmother had just died.

Their mother.

The woman who raised Robert until he was ten years old.

He almost couldn't believe it.

This woman had given Robert so much of her life. So much love. So much care and education and everything she possibly could. She had invested years raising him, believing in him, hoping he would make something of his life.

Now she was gone.

And here was Robert, on the brink of bankruptcy.

He had failed. He couldn't even afford to fly home for her funeral.

He cried for several days.

But then something shifted.

He made a decision: From this moment forward, he would always ask for the value of the services he provided. He would ask for payment upfront. He would get paid. And then deliver the service.

That was the moment Robert started tracking his finances.

ROBERT'S LIFE-CHANGING WEEKLY HABIT

He didn't just start tracking his finances monthly. He tracked them weekly.

Every single dollar that came in. Every single dollar that went out. He tracked everything.

And every single week he would sit down and ask himself two questions:

1. How could he improve his income this week?

2. How could he reduce his costs this week?

Fifty-two times per year. Every single week, without fail.

It wasn't easy at first. He was starting from zero—actually, worse than zero. He started from absolute desperation.

Robert picked up every gig he could find. One job was translating every description of museum artwork in Spain, from Spanish to English. If you visit certain museums in Spain today, Robert's translations are still there!

The first month, he made around $300 in profit after all expenses.

The second month, maybe about $700.

Month three, $1,800.

The numbers kept growing. Every single month.

And then, exactly one year after that phone call from Europe—one year after being down to his last $100—Robert pocketed $17,000 in profit, in one single month.

This is the power of what we are teaching you in this chapter.

Measure your income. Measure your expenses. Create your balance sheet. Track your P&L. And then every single week—not just monthly, but weekly—ask yourself: How can I improve my income? How can I reduce my costs? Or both?

If you do this consistently, you can make 50 improvements throughout the year.

By the end of one year, you'll be in a place that's completely different from where you started.

That's what happened to Robert. From $300 per month to $17,000 per month in one year.

Not because he got lucky, nor because of some secret strategy. But because he finally started measuring what mattered, tracking his progress weekly, taking every opportunity he could find, and taking 100% responsibility for his financial situation.

And just to be clear, though Robert kept asking himself, "How can I reduce my costs?" Every week, the reality is that his costs were already low, and he focused 10X more on how he could increase his income. A proportion which he still keeps to this day, because he realizes we only have one life to live, so he was way less concerned with skimping on a vacation, but 10X more concerned about "How can I make more next month?"

WHY WE DON'T LEARN THIS IN SCHOOL

Here's something that's quite annoying. The information we're about to share with you—understanding balance sheets, profit and loss statements, assets versus liabilities—should be mandatory learning in every high school in the country.

This isn't advanced financial theory. This is basic financial literacy. It's knowledge that every person needs to manage their money effectively and build wealth over time.

But for whatever reason, our education system doesn't teach it. You can graduate with honors, get multiple degrees, and still have no idea how to read a balance sheet or understand real EBITDA (Earnings Before Interest, Taxes, Depreciation, and Amortization).

Why wouldn't you learn this in schools? This is such an important part of life. It should be mandatory.

We've worked with millionaires who never put together a personal balance sheet until we showed them how. Smart, successful people who built businesses and accumulated wealth, but never formally tracked their wealth journey the way we're going to show you.

So if you're reading this and thinking, "I should already know this," don't beat yourself up. You're not alone. Most people don't know this stuff because they were never taught.

The good news? You're about to learn it right now.

WHAT IS A BALANCE SHEET?

Let's start with the basics. A balance sheet is a financial snapshot that shows three things:

- **Assets** – what you own
- **Liabilities** – what you owe
- **Net Worth** – the difference between the two

That's it. It's remarkably simple, but very powerful.

If you have $150,000 in assets and $80,000 in liabilities, your net worth is $70,000. Simple math. This number tells you exactly where you stand financially.

UNDERSTANDING ASSETS VS LIABILITIES

Much of what we've learned about thinking clearly about assets and liabilities came from Robert Kiyosaki's books, such as *Rich Dad Poor Dad*.

If you haven't read it, put it on your list. It's one of those books that fundamentally changes how you think about money.

Kiyosaki tells the story of two fictional father figures in his life. One was highly educated—a reader, an intellectual—but lacked financial literacy. That's why he never became financially successful. The other, the "rich dad," understood wealth, assets, liabilities, and how money really works.

Here's Kiyosaki's simple but profound distinction:

- **An asset puts money in your pocket**
- **A liability takes money out of your pocket**

By this definition, your primary residence isn't technically an asset—even though it shows up on your balance sheet as one. Why? Because it costs you money every month in mortgage payments, insurance, taxes, and maintenance. And... it doesn't generate income.

A profitable rental property you own? That's an asset, because it generates rental income.

Now, we're not saying you shouldn't own your home. Most people should. But it's important to understand the distinction. True wealth comes from accumulating income-generating assets, not just things that have value on paper.

THE CASH FLOW GAME

Speaking of Robert Kiyosaki, as a quick parenthesis, he created a game called "Cash Flow" that teaches these principles in a fun, interactive way. You can play it online for free, or buy the board game version.

The game has two parts:

The Rat Race: This is where your passive income has not yet exceeded your recurring expenses. You're working to pay your bills. You're stuck in the cycle of trading time for money.

You keep playing in the rat race until your passive income is higher than your expenses. The moment you achieve that, you get promoted to the next level.

The Fast Track: Once your passive income exceeds your expenses, you move to the fast track—where new opportunities open up and your wealth can grow exponentially. There are bigger opportunities here, and you have the financial freedom to benefit from them.

Do these two descriptions sound at all familiar? That's because they're exactly what the first two parts of this book are about—getting you to the fast track where you can deploy capital, buy assets, and generate passive income that significantly exceeds your expenses. (It's also what we do for our clients at Elkridge Advisors).

We recommend playing the game if you get a chance. It makes these concepts tangible and exemplifies the path to wealth in under 30 minutes.

CREATING YOUR PERSONAL BALANCE SHEET

All right, let's build your actual balance sheet.

A simple spreadsheet can work perfectly, though we do recommend something in the cloud, like Google Sheets or Office 365, so you can update and access it from anywhere.

Or use the Balance Sheet Template or App we link to in the Resources section at the end of the book.

Assets	
Savings	**Amount**
Cash on Hand	$100,000
BOA Secure Deposit	$100,000
Assets	**Value**
2023 Ford Explorer	$40,000
2025 Microsoft Surface	$2,000
Stocks	**Value**
S&P500	$143,000
NVDA	$55,000
Real Estate	**Equity**
123 Main Street, NY, Condo	$90,000
27 Pleasant Drive, NY, House	$210,000
Companies	**Equity**
Joe's Car Wash	$800,000
Martha's Coffee Shop	$700,000
Total Assets	$2,240,000

Liabilities	
Personal	**Amount**
Student Loan	$100,000
Credit Card One	$10,000
Credit Card Two	$7,000
Car Loan	$13,000
Real Estate Debt	**Amount**
123 Main Street, NY, Condo	$120,000
27 Pleasant Drive, NY, House	$130,000
Business Debt	**Amount**
Joe's Car Wash	$400,000
Martha's Coffee Shop	$800,000
Total Liabilities	$1,580,000

Current Net Worth	**$660,000**

Graphic: Balance Sheet Example

Here's how to use it:

STEP 1: LIST ALL YOUR ASSETS

Go through each category and write down everything you own that has value:

- **Cash & Checking Accounts:** Add up all your bank balances
- **Savings Accounts:** Include any emergency funds or savings
- **Retirement Accounts:** 401(k), IRA, pension values
- **Investment Accounts:** Brokerage accounts, stocks, crypto, bonds
- **Real Estate:** Current market value of any property you own
- **Business Equity:** If you own a business, estimate its current value (Typically 3x EBITDA)
- **Vehicles:** Current market value (not what you paid)
- **Other Assets:** Valuable possessions like jewelry, art, collectibles

Be honest. Don't inflate values to make yourself feel better. Use current market values, not what you wish something was worth.

STEP 2: LIST ALL YOUR LIABILITIES

Now write down everything you owe:

- **Mortgage Balance:** What you still owe on any properties
- **Car Loans:** Outstanding balance on vehicle loans

- **Student Loans:** Total amount still owed
- **Credit Card Debt:** Combined balance across all cards
- **Personal Loans:** Money owed to friends, family, or lenders
- **Other Liabilities:** Any other obligations

Again, be ruthlessly honest. This is for you, not for social media. Nobody else needs to see this.

STEP 3: CALCULATE YOUR NET WORTH

Total up all your assets. Total up all your liabilities. Subtract liabilities from assets.

That's your current net worth.

How do you feel looking at that number?

If it's negative, don't panic. Many people start this journey with a negative net worth. What matters is that you know the number and you're committed to improving it.

If it's positive, congratulations. Now you have a baseline to exceed.

YOUR MONTHLY P&L

Your balance sheet shows where you stand. Your P&L shows how you're moving.

A personal P&L is also simple. It tracks three things each month:

- **Income** – All money coming in (salary, side hustles, rental income, dividends, royalties)

- **Expenses** – All money going out (rent/mortgage, food, utilities, entertainment, etc.)
- **Cash Flow** – Income minus expenses (your monthly surplus or deficit)

If you make $6,000 per month and spend $4,500, your cash flow is $1,500. That's $1,500 you can save or invest each month to grow your net worth.

If you make $6,000 and spend $6,500, your cash flow is -$500. You're going backwards. That needs to change.

Year 2026	January	February	March
Active Income			
Full-Time Job	$8,000	$8,000	$8,700
Side Gigs	$2,000	$2,200	$1,500
Passive Income			
Joe's Car Wash	$7,000	$8,000	$9,000
Martha's Coffee Shop	$3,000	$3,500	$4,000
Total Income	**$20,000**	**$21,700**	**$23,200**
Expenses			
Taxes	$7,000	$7,500	$8,000
Mortgage	$1,250	$1,250	$1,250
Utilities	$500	$500	$500
Car Lease	$750	$750	$750
Groceries	$900	$900	$900
Miscellaneous	$600	$600	$600
Total Expenses	**$13,000**	**$13,500**	**$14,000**
Monthly Cash Flow	$7,000	$8,200	$9,200

Graphic: P&L Example.

Track this monthly. Create a simple spreadsheet with these three sections.

Update it at the end of each month. Watch the trends.

Are your expenses creeping up? Are you finding new income sources? Is your cash flow improving or declining?

This awareness is gold. It's much harder to make good financial decisions without knowing these numbers.

You can also use the editable P&L Template and App we link to in the Resources section at the end of the book.

THE POWER OF REGULAR MEASUREMENT

Create your personal balance sheet and monthly P&L right now.

Not tomorrow. Not next week. Right now.

It'll take you 30-60 minutes to pull together all the numbers. Do it.

Then commit to updating your balance sheet once per month and reviewing your financial position once per week.

Here's what we recommend:

Monthly: Update your full balance sheet and P&L. Track your net worth, your income, your expenses, your cash flow. Put this on your calendar for the first of every month.

Weekly: Review your numbers and ask yourself two questions:

- How can I improve my income this week?
- How can I reduce my costs this week?

This doesn't have to take long. Ten minutes. Fifteen minutes. But do it every single week.

Why weekly? Because it keeps your finances front of mind. It prevents you from going on autopilot. It forces you to actively look for opportunities to improve.

Some people track daily. That's fine if it works for you. But weekly reviews and monthly updates are the minimum we recommend if you're serious about building wealth.

And here's what you'll discover: the simple act of measuring these numbers will change your behavior. You'll start thinking differently about purchases. You'll look for ways that actually increase your income. You'll be more intentional about where your money flows.

Remember: What you measure tends to improve. What you focus on grows. What you neglect tends to deplete.

THE PATH FORWARD

Your personal balance sheet is the foundation of everything else in this book.

In the next chapter, we'll talk about choosing your path—career or entrepreneurship. And in the subsequent chapters, 3-10, we'll show you more of the powerful strategies we recommend you follow to get to $300,000 in assets.

It all starts here. With this one simple document: Your Personal Balance Sheet.

This is your financial GPS for the wealth journey you're about to go on.

ACTION STEPS

1. **Create your personal balance sheet today.** List all assets and all liabilities. Calculate your current net worth.

2. **Set up a monthly P&L tracker.** Record this month's income, expenses, and cash flow.

3. **Schedule a recurring monthly reminder** to update both documents on the first of each month.

4. **Schedule a recurring weekly reminder** to review your numbers and ask: "How can I improve my income? How can I reduce my costs?"

5. **(Optional)** Play the Cash Flow game to reinforce these concepts.

CHAPTER 2

CHOOSE YOUR PATH

People ask us all the time: "Should I be an entrepreneur or should I focus on my career?"

An understandable question. The entrepreneurial dream is everywhere. Social media makes it look glamorous. The freedom, the control, the potential for unlimited income. Who wouldn't want that?

But here's what nobody tells you: entrepreneurship isn't the only path to wealth. It's not even the fastest path for most people. And it's definitely not the right path for everyone.

This chapter is about making one of the most important decisions of your life: choosing how you're going to build wealth. Career or business? Employee or entrepreneur?

The answer isn't what you think. And it matters more than you realize.

THE TRUTH ABOUT ENTREPRENEURSHIP

Robert has a confession: he never wanted to be an entrepreneur. He wanted to be an engineer. That's it. He loves building things. He loves solving technical problems. He's geeky about systems and processes. He wanted to work for a great company, do excellent engineering work, and build a comfortable life.

But Robert couldn't find a company that aligned with his values.

This was about 20 years ago in semi-communist Romania. The work environment was sub-optimal. Employees were treated like replaceable cogs in a machine. If you didn't perform exactly as expected, you were replaced. No respect for the individual. No care for employee wellbeing. Just production, production, production.

He tried. Multiple times. Different companies. Same story.

Eventually, he realized he had two choices: compromise his values and just make money, or build something with the kind of work environment he believed in.

So he became an entrepreneur by (what he felt was) necessity, not by choice.

Now, fast forward to today. Robert has built multiple million-dollar businesses. He's in the top 0.1% of entrepreneurs globally. He's helped dozens of other entrepreneurs scale past seven figures. By almost any measure, he's a very successful business owner.

And here's the irony: Today, Robert would be wealthier if he had stayed an employee.

Let that sink in for a moment.

WHY EMPLOYEES BUILD MORE WEALTH

This isn't just Robert's story. It's statistically provable.

Most wealthy people in America aren't entrepreneurs. They're highly skilled professionals who climbed the career ladder, earned excellent incomes, and invested wisely.

The vast majority of millionaires are lawyers, accountants, doctors, engineers, marketing executives, and other professionals. They never started a business. They just got really good at their craft, earned strong incomes, kept their expenses within their means, and invested the difference.

Why? Because when you're an employee, every dollar you earn above your living expenses can go directly into wealth-building assets. Real estate. Stock market. Index funds. Retirement accounts.

When you're an entrepreneur, you reinvest every dollar you earn back into the business. You're constantly plowing profits into growth, hiring, equipment, marketing. That's how businesses scale. But it's also why entrepreneurs often have less liquid wealth than successful professionals earning the same amount.

Robert made over $10 million by the time he was 31. Statistically, almost no one achieves that. Only 4% of businesses ever pass $1 million in annual revenue. Robert achieved that multiple times, with different companies, in different sectors, and on different continents.

And yet... if he had taken that same drive, that same work ethic, that same creativity, and applied it to climbing the corporate ladder, he'd have an even higher net worth today.

Don't get us wrong, this isn't a complaint. We've learned to love what we do. We fell in love with the freedom to dream, with the ability to build teams and systems that work 100% without our involvement.

But we're telling you this because nobody else will: From a purely financial perspective, your path doesn't determine your wealth. Your execution does.

THE INSTAGRAM LIE

You know what you see on social media? Entrepreneurs flaunting their lifestyles. The cars. The houses. The "passive income." The "freedom."

You know what you don't see? Millions of high-earning professionals living quietly, building substantial wealth year after year without the drama or risk of business ownership.

There's a reason for that: employees don't get likes.

A surgeon making $500,000 a year and investing $300,000 of it isn't posting about it on Instagram. But over 10-20 years, they're building serious wealth. And they're doing it without the stress of payroll, the risk of business failure, or the constant hustle of entrepreneurship.

The truth is this: you can become wealthy doing anything if you become really good at it—and if you make smart financial decisions.

Writers. Teachers. Engineers. Plumbers. Accountants. Marketers. Sales professionals. It doesn't matter. Pick your path. Get excellent at it. Earn well. Invest wisely. Repeat.

That's the formula. The vehicle doesn't matter.

WHY BECOME AN ENTREPRENEUR?

Given everything we just said, you might be thinking: "Why would anyone choose entrepreneurship?"

Fair question. Here are the only good reasons to become an entrepreneur:

1. YOU'RE NATURALLY A GENERALIST

Entrepreneurship requires you to be good at a little bit of everything. Marketing. Sales. Operations. Finance. HR. Customer service. Strategy. You don't need to be an expert in any one area, but you need to understand them all.

If you're someone who gets bored doing the same thing every day, who loves variety, who enjoys wearing multiple hats, entrepreneurship might be for you.

But if you love specializing? If you want to become the absolute best at one specific thing? Stay in your career. Specialize. Master your craft. You'll be happier and likely wealthier.

2. VALUES DON'T MATCH

This was Robert's reason. He couldn't find companies that treated people the way he believed they should be treated.

If you're in a similar situation—you've tried the corporate world, you've given it an honest shot across 5-10 years, and you just can't make it work—then entrepreneurship might be your path.

But be honest with yourself. Is it really about values? Or are you just running from something uncomfortable?

3. YOU HAVE A SPECIFIC VISION

Some people have a product, service, or vision that simply doesn't exist in the world. If you're compelled to create something new, something that solves a problem you're passionate about—that's a legitimate reason to start a business.

But make sure it's about the vision, not the lifestyle.

4. YOU DON'T WANT TO WORK FOR SOMEONE

There are many careers where you can literally start on your own and carve a path for yourself. Arts, such as painting or sculpting; home services, such as renovations or electric; writing, books or news, filmmaking, photography, and the list goes on and on, with hundreds of things you can do on your own or with a small team.

In this case, be very honest with yourself, and make sure it's about your desire to do more with the freedom you have, and not about ego or arrogance, such as "no one tells me what to do."

WHY NOT TO BECOME AN ENTREPRENEUR

On the flip side, here are terrible reasons to start a business:

"I want to make more money." Statistically, you'll probably make less. At least for the first 5-10 years.

"I want to be my own boss." You'll have more bosses than ever: customers, employees, investors, vendors, the market itself.

"I want freedom and flexibility." Most entrepreneurs work more hours than employees, not fewer. Especially in the first 5-10 years.

"I want power over others." This is a character issue. Fix that first.

If any of these are your primary motivations, stop. Choose a career instead. You'll be happier and wealthier.

FINDING YOUR CORE GENIUS

How do you actually choose your path?

Let's do an exercise. It's simple but powerful. This is how you find what we call your "core genius"—the intersection of what you should be doing with your life.

Here's how it works:

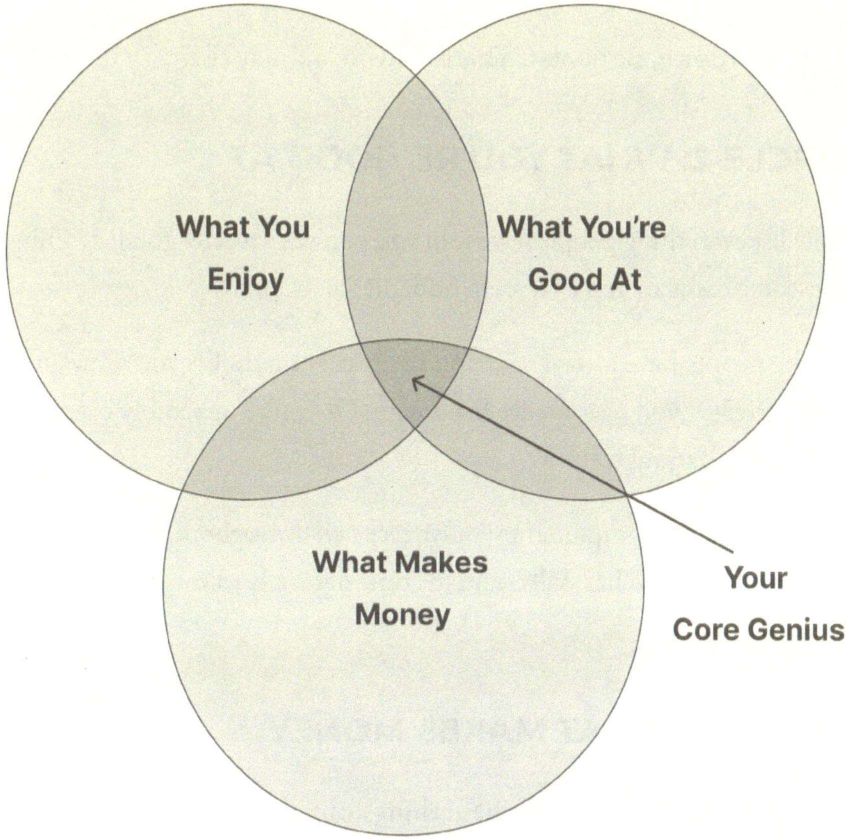

Graphic: Your Core Genius.

CIRCLE 1: WHAT YOU ENJOY

Make a list of everything you genuinely enjoy doing. Not what you think you should enjoy. Not what your parents want you to enjoy. What you actually enjoy.

Maybe it's analyzing data. Maybe it's talking to people. Maybe it's creating content. Maybe it's building things with your hands. Maybe it's teaching others.

Write it all down. Be honest. This is for you, nobody else.

CIRCLE 2: WHAT YOU'RE GOOD AT

Now list everything people have told you you're naturally good at. Things that come easily to you that seem difficult for others.

Maybe people have always said you're great at math. Or you're naturally persuasive. Or you have an eye for design. Or you're incredibly organized. Or you're a natural teacher.

Think about the compliments you've received throughout your life. What patterns emerge? What skills seem to come naturally to you without much effort?

CIRCLE 3: WHAT MAKES MONEY

Now research how each of these things can generate income. And be specific about earning potential.

If you're good at math, you could be:

- A data analyst ($70K-120K)

- A financial analyst ($80K-150K)
- A math tutor ($50-150/hour)
- A quant trader ($150K-500K+)
- A math teacher ($45K-65K)

Do this for everything on your lists. Research salaries. Look at business models. Understand the economic realities of each path.

IMPORTANT: WRITE EACH LIST SEPARATELY

Don't try to figure out the intersection while you're brainstorming. Just dump everything onto paper first, one list at a time. Then step back and look at all three lists together.

Where do they overlap?

What activities show up in all three circles? That's your core genius. That's where you should focus.

CONSIDER YOUR NETWORK

Here's one more factor that Patrick always emphasizes: Who's in your network?

Do you have connections in a specific industry? Do you know people who could mentor you, partner with you, or open doors for you?

Sometimes the fastest path to success isn't the "perfect" path on paper—it's the path where you have relationships that can accelerate your results.

If your uncle is a successful commercial real estate investor and he's willing to mentor you, that might be worth more than choosing a field you're theoretically more passionate about.

If you spent five years in medical device sales and you know everyone in the industry, maybe that's your lane—even if it wasn't your childhood dream.

Relationships compound. Leverage them.

A FRAMEWORK FOR DECIDING

Here's a simple decision framework:

Choose a career path if:

- You love specialization and mastery of one craft
- You value stability and predictable income
- You want to invest your money rather than reinvest it in operations
- You enjoy being part of a team without managing it
- You're motivated by clear advancement paths
- You want to separate work from personal identity

Choose entrepreneurship if:

- You're naturally a generalist and easily bored
- You have a specific vision that doesn't exist in the market
- You can't find work environments that align with your values
- You're willing to trade short-term income for long-term equity

- You're comfortable with uncertainty and risk (a lot of risk)
- You want to build systems and lead teams

Neither path is better. They're just different. And both can lead to substantial wealth if executed well.

A WORD ABOUT CAREER CHANGES

Here's something else nobody tells you: you can change your mind.

We know people who spent 15 years as engineers, then started consulting businesses. We know entrepreneurs who sold their companies and joined corporations in executive roles. We know corporate vice presidents who quit to become real estate investors.

Your first choice isn't your forever choice.

Start somewhere. Build skills. Learn. Earn. Network. Then reassess every few years. Are you happy? Are you growing? Are you building wealth? Is this still aligned with who you're becoming?

If yes, keep going. If not, pivot.

The worst decision is no decision. Paralysis kills more dreams than failure ever will.

SET YOUR GOALS

Once you've chosen your path—career or entrepreneurship—it's time to set specific goals.

Not vague aspirations like "be successful" or "make good money." Actual, measurable goals, with timelines.

If you're on a career path:

- What position do you want to reach in 1 year? 3 years? 5 years?
- What salary do you want by those milestones?
- What skills do you need to get there?
- What certifications or credentials would help you advance?
- What percentage of your income will you invest?

If you're on an entrepreneurial path:

- What revenue do you want to hit in one year? Three years? Five years?
- Who are your ideal clients and why would they buy specifically from you?
- How will you make sure your clients get outstanding value for money, fall in love with your products or services, and recommend you to others?
- What people will you need? In what roles? How much will you need to pay them?
- What systems need to be in place?

We're big believers in dreaming. It's what has kept us going these last 20 years. We've always had very vivid visions of a better future. It almost makes us cry thinking about it...

A boy that was feeding chickens and walking cows, generated over $10M with clients in 17 countries...

Whatever you want, it CAN happen. Write down your vision, in as much detail as you can, and then get to work. You don't need a 3-hour morning routine. Just get to work.

MANIFEST YOUR FUTURE

Now that you know where you want to be, let's stack the Universe in your favor for getting you there!

A number of years ago, Patrick was at perhaps one of the lowest points of his life.

He'd just lost who he thought at the time was the love of his life. He was suffering from low energy and was down to $5,000 per month in income. Coming from $30,000 a month, it was quite drastic. He'd lost clients due to situations which were completely out of his control, and had a number of consulting contracts end at the same time.

The timing couldn't be worse. Patrick had just separated from a business partner who was mentoring him in mergers and acquisitions. He essentially stole from Patrick—what should have been a $2.5 million commission, turned into a fraction of that years later, and only after significant attorney fees.

However, as you can imagine, these events provided the best education and lessons money can buy, and placed him *exactly* where he is today: Patrick would not have started Elkridge Advisors without this experience.

However, at the time, he wasn't yet a highly seasoned M&A strategist. and had no direction. No path forward. No idea what he was going to do next.

Patrick was lost.

And then, within a couple weeks of each other, three separate people came into his life with the same message.

They were very similar recommendations from people he deeply respected. One was his kickboxing instructor—a spiritually elevated friend from Oregon who was also a business coach. All three said essentially the same thing:

"Patrick, you need to learn how to talk to your subconscious mind."

They all recommended the same message, which can be found and best summarized in this book: *The Power of Your Subconscious Mind* by Joseph Murphy.

Patrick read it, and started implementing what it taught.

Within three months, everything changed.

The Elkridge Path business model? It came to him. Robert reached out to Patrick out of the blue.

Opportunities he wasn't even seeking started appearing. The answers were coming to him. He wasn't searching for them.

For a period of about 1.5 months, Patrick started to make progress and decisions on his new path and direction. He kept seeing the 11:11 number pairing everywhere—on clocks, receipts, license plates. He didn't know what it meant for the first couple weeks. But then he learned that in the spiritual world it's a sign you are in a manifestation flow. It's a signal for high conscious alignment with the universe. It's a sign you're on the right path. Even though you feel you're at a crossroads, like you don't know where to go, the universe is showing you you are on the right path.

But here's what most people get wrong about manifestation and visualization.

WHERE VISUALIZATION BREAKS DOWN

Most people think manifestation is about affirmations. They stand in front of a mirror and repeat: "I am wealthy. I am successful. I am confident." (And by golly, people *like* me).

And then... nothing happens.

Why?

Because visualization without emotion and gratitude does not allow you to truly manifest.

Your subconscious mind is 40 million times more powerful than your conscious mind. It doesn't process language the way your conscious mind does. It responds to feelings, emotions, and vivid sensory experiences.

When you visualize your success without truly *feeling* it in your body, you're wasting your time. You're missing one of the core elements of the law of attraction.

But there's another very important element: your current beliefs around getting what you want.

Everything that's in alignment with your frequency is already trying to reach you. But if they're not reaching you, it may not be because you're not vibrating at the correct frequency. It's because your definitions and beliefs are preventing them from reaching you.

The true secret of the law of attraction is not *only* to learn to attract what you want, but to learn how to let go of what you *don't* want, in order to let in what you *do* want.

PATRICK'S THREE-PHASE PROCESS

Let's walk you exactly through Patrick's process to attract what he wants in life. This is the process that transformed his life in only three months.

PHASE ONE: ENTER A MEDITATIVE STATE

First, you need to get your brain into an alpha state—and ideally, into theta.

Patrick uses a combination of techniques from various teachers: Joe Dispenza's methods from *Becoming Supernatural*, Jose Silva's Ultra Mind Method, and Patrick's own adaptations.

Here's the process:

Start with controlled breathing. Deep breaths. Get out of your mind and into your body.

Then do what Patrick calls a "drop-in." Start at the top of your head and slowly move down, visualizing every muscle, every ligament, the blood cells flowing, the temperature, the tingling sensations. Focus on your scalp, then your forehead, your eyes, your cheeks. After visualizing each muscle group, consciously relax it and shut it down.

Go from the top of your head all the way to the bottom of your feet. If you do this correctly, you'll literally stop feeling your body. Your mind will be completely relaxed. Your body will be completely relaxed. You won't be thinking about the crazy things happening in your life.

Patrick used a headband called Muse (about $300). It's a mental biofeedback system that measures your brain activity. When your brain reaches a certain state of calm, it chirps at you. It helped him learn what theta state actually feels like.

PHASE TWO: CREATE YOUR HAPPY STATE

Once you're in that deeply relaxed state, create a vivid mental environment.

Patrick's environment is a field in the mountains. There's a creek running through short grass. There's a small pedestrian bridge over the creek. Beautiful mountains rise in the background. Birds are tweeting. The wind is blowing slightly—you can see the wind moving through the hay and feel the breeze on your skin.

He spends about 5 minutes here just in awe of the scene, and gets lost in the experience. In the middle of the field in the ground, there's a door. He walks over to the door and opens it. There's a stairwell with 20 stairs. He walks down the stairs, counting from 20 to 0. By the time he reaches the bottom, if he followed everything in the process, Patrick finds himself in a very relaxed meditative state where his subconscious is open to new suggestive ideas and concepts.

This is basically self-hypnosis. It's the same as a deep meditative state. Different teachers use different methods, but this is what works for Patrick.

PHASE THREE: FEEL GRATITUDE

This is where the real work happens.

Once you're in that alpha or theta state, you start visualizing your future as if it's already happening. And this is absolutely key.

Not as a distant goal. Not as something you *want*. **As something you're *experiencing right now and have gratitude for.*** This is critical. You cannot think of it as something you want, because then you are telling the universe that you don't have it.

Swiss Researchers (Gisin's Group) performed a ground breaking experiment that proves the universe mirrors your beliefs. It was conducted in 1997 and called the twin photon experiment. They took a single photon, cut it in two so it would have identical properties. They then used fiber optic cables and sent one photon 7 miles in one direction of the cable, and the other 7 miles in the other direction. (Source:).

Then they would start the experiment and induce some kind of stimulant on one of the photons, in this case, Photon A. What they found is that Photon B, which did NOT receive the stimulation, experienced the same exact reaction and impact at the same exact atomic time, as Photon A. There was no delay in time between stimulant and reaction in the unaffected photon, and the experience was exactly the same.

This is called *entanglement.* The photons were entangled with one another.

The quantum field is neutral and it can only act on what we give it to work with. When we ask for a prayer to be fulfilled, we are telling the quantum field it is not true. We're saying, "Please let this happen!" So the field will reflect that it's not happening, which is very different than having gratitude for it already being here.

Patrick visualized meeting his children or his future wife at the dock of his future yacht. Walking down to the boat. Pulling into the Bahamas. Docking. Swimming with them. Enjoying dinner together. Going spear fishing off the back of the yacht. Having extreme gratitude for all of it already being here.

He repeats this for his house on the lake, the house on the beach, flying in his personal jet. And...this is very important...FEELING THE EMOTIONS of gratitude and joy as he visualizes his "current life".

Patrick will visualize his business. He will see himself helping clients generate $300,000+ per year in passive income per each business he helps them acquire. He watches them get excited. He feels their gratitude. He experiences the satisfaction of delivering massive value, and he even envisions how their lives improve from working with us.

When Patrick does this correctly, he'll get goosebumps. Literal shivers running through his body.

That's the key: the emotion of gratitude..

You see, your brain doesn't know the difference between a vividly imagined experience and a real one. When you put yourself into the emotion of your future—when you truly *feel* the gratitude—your subconscious mind goes to work and the universe delivers it to you.

Literally, while you sleep, your subconscious solves problems. It makes decisions. It attracts opportunities you would never have found consciously. This new reality you want already exists, you just have to match the frequency and vibration of already having it. The universe will have no choice but to deliver your envisioned future to you.

The more you can stay in that theta state when meditating, visualizing, and feeling those positive emotions, the more manifestation occurs.

A PRACTICAL EXAMPLE

Here's how this worked recently.

Early in 2025, Patrick was scaling Elkridge Advisors. He'd finally figured out the sales and marketing piece. But he was starting to get a little stressed because he didn't know how he was going to scale the delivery and operations side for so many new clients. He didn't know how he was going to fulfill the promises he was making to clients who were coming so quickly. So Patrick started to let his foot off the gas to focus on current clients.

One Saturday night, as the pressure started to weigh heavily on his mind, Patrick decided to meditate. He reached theta state. Before going to sleep, he posed a question to his subconscious: "How do I solve this scaling problem? I have a huge opportunity in front of me, but I just don't know if I have the resources and capabilities to do this right."

Then he let it go. He trusted his subconscious to work on it while he slept.

The next morning, Robert reached out to Patrick.

We'd known each other from Patrick's podcast, *High Performance CEO.* Patrick referred clients to Robert over the years. But he didn't consciously connect Robert's outreach to his meditation the night before. Not at first.

Over the next week or two, we had Zoom call after Zoom call. We got more and more excited. Patrick hired Robert's company to systematize his processes. Suddenly we both realized that 1+1 equals 3 if we fully partnered on Elkridge, and we became business partners.

That's manifestation in action. We still get goosebumps even now as we re-read this and edit the book for publication.

THE BOOKS THAT CHANGED EVERYTHING

If you want to go deeper on this, here are the resources that transformed our understanding:

- *The Power of Your Subconscious Mind,* by Joseph Murphy
- *Becoming Supernatural,* by Joe Dispenza

- *The Silva Mind Control Method,* by Jose Silva

We've read probably 20 different books on manifestation at this point. They all point to the same truth: you must retrain your subconscious mind to overcome prior conditioning and learn how to correctly manifest through visualization and positive emotions. You might get lucky and succeed without the meditation work, but in the long run, it's harder to be successful without doing this work.

WHEN IT WORKS AND WHEN IT DOESN'T

When we fall away from meditative practices—when we let stress take over, when a relationship ends, when issues pile up—we veer away from our goals. The manifestation stops working.

Consistency is everything.

You can't do this once and expect miracles. You need to practice. Daily, if possible. At minimum, several times per week.

But when you do it consistently? When you truly commit to getting into that alpha and theta state and visualizing your future with genuine emotion?

The results are undeniable.

WHY THIS BELONGS HERE

You might be wondering why we're talking about meditation and manifestation in a book about business acquisition and wealth building.

Here's why: your mindset determines your results.

You can have the best strategy in the world. You can know exactly how to find deals, how to finance them, how to automate operations. But if your subconscious mind is programmed with fear, scarcity, and doubt, you'll sabotage yourself at every turn.

As business coaches and consultants for over 20 years, we've seen it happen over and over again.

People may have all the knowledge they need but can't pull the trigger on executing the plan. People who find perfect acquisition targets but talk themselves out of it. People who build successful businesses but can't enjoy them because they're consumed by anxiety.

The external strategies in this book work. But they work best when your internal state is aligned.

Before you do the Three Circles exercise we described earlier in this chapter, we recommend getting into a meditative state. Do the visualization work. Calm your nervous system. Approach the exercise from a place of abundance, not scarcity.

The path you choose matters. But the state of mind you bring to that path matters even more.

Remember: this isn't woo-woo nonsense. This is practical neuroscience applied to wealth building. Your subconscious mind is either working for you or against you. This process ensures it's working for you.

IT'S NOT YOUR PATH, IT'S YOUR COMMITMENT

Let's end this chapter with the most important point:

Your success has almost nothing to do with whether you choose a career or entrepreneurship. It has everything to do with your commitment to excellence in whatever path you choose.

A mediocre entrepreneur will struggle. A mediocre employee will plateau. But an excellent entrepreneur or an excellent employee? Both will build substantial wealth.

So choose your path based on fit, not perceived prestige or income potential. Choose the path that aligns with your nature, your values, and your core genius.

Then commit fully. Become excellent. Execute relentlessly.

That's how wealth is built.

ACTION STEPS

Choose Your Path:

1. **Enter a meditative state before strategic planning.** Before you start the exercises below, spend 10-15 minutes calming your mind. Do deep breathing. Get into your body. Approach these decisions from a place of abundance.

2. **Complete the Three Circles exercise.** List everything in each circle before looking for overlaps. Circle 1: What you enjoy. Circle 2: What you're naturally good at. Circle 3: What makes money. Be thorough. Take your time.

3. **Research the earning potential of activities in your overlap zone.** Be realistic about timelines and requirements. Look at actual salaries, business revenue potential, and growth trajectories. Write down specific numbers.

4. **List everyone in your network who could help you in potential career paths.** Consider their influence on your decision. Who can open doors? Who can mentor you? Who has

already succeeded in areas you're considering?

5. **Make a decision: career path or entrepreneurial?** Write it down with today's date. Commit to it. You can always change later, but make a clear choice now.

6. **Set three specific, measurable goals for your chosen path with 1-year, 3-year, and 5-year timelines.** Not vague aspirations. Actual numbers. Specific positions. Concrete milestones. Write them down.

Manifest Your Future:

1. **Buy one book on manifestation.** Start with *The Power of Your Subconscious Mind* by Joseph Murphy or *Becoming Supernatural* by Joe Dispenza. Read either of them this month.

2. **Learn a basic meditation technique.** We recommend listening to Joe Dispenze or Jose Silva and incorporating their techniques. Start with 10 minutes daily. Work up to 20-30 minutes once you're comfortable. Consistency matters more than duration.

3. **Create your happy place.** Write down a vivid description of a peaceful environment where you'll begin your visualizations. Include all five senses: what you see, hear, feel, smell, and taste. Make it real in your mind.

4. **Practice the drop-in technique.** Once per day this week, spend 15 minutes doing the body scan from your head to your feet. Relax and "shut down" each muscle group as you go. Notice when your body fully relaxes.

5. **Visualize one specific goal from your Three Circles exercise.**

Spend 5-10 minutes each day visualizing yourself already having achieved it. This is critical: don't visualize wanting it or working toward it. Visualize experiencing it right now. Feel the emotions. Experience the sensations. Get goosebumps. Make it viscerally real.

6. **Track your meditation and visualization practice.** Note in your calendar or journal every time you meditate and visualize. Track for 30 days and observe what changes in your life, your opportunities, and your mindset.

7. **Schedule a quarterly review.** Put it in your calendar now. Every 90 days, review your goals, assess your progress, and make adjustments. Check if your path still feels right. Pivot if necessary.

Remember: Choosing your path is both strategic and spiritual. Use Robert's framework to make smart decisions based on your skills and market opportunities. Use Patrick's manifestation practice to align your subconscious mind with your goals. Both are necessary. Strategy without mindset leads to self-sabotage. Mindset without strategy leads to fairytale thinking.

If you'd like access to Your Core Genius Worksheet, guided meditation playlists, or other tools, just follow the link in the Resources section of this book.

CHAPTER 3

LEARN TO FULLY UNDERSTAND OTHERS

There was a period in Robert's life when he had a 100% close rate in sales.

Not 90%. Not 95%. One hundred percent.

If you got on a call with Robert, you became a client. This happened every single time. For six straight months.

The most memorable example? An eight-minute call where someone who explicitly didn't want to work with "yet another marketing agency" gave him verbal approval for a $168,000 contract. Robert sent them paperwork that same day. They signed and paid immediately.

How did Robert achieve this? Was he using manipulative tactics? Was he lying or overselling? Was he taking advantage of people?

None of that.

He did it by mastering one skill that most people never even think about: understanding personality types.

Specifically, Robert learned the DISC personality framework. And once he understood it deeply, he could identify someone's dominant personality type within the first minute of conversation. Sometimes in the first 30 seconds.

That skill changed everything.

THIS SKILL MATTERS MORE THAN YOU THINK

Understanding personality types isn't just useful for sales. It's useful for literally everything in your life. That's what this chapter is about. But first, we'll tell you about how Robert got there.

THE PATH TO MASTERY

Here's something important about Robert's journey: he didn't stop at "good enough."

Throughout his career, whenever he started a new role—whether it was engineering, sales, marketing, or anything else—he committed to becoming a top performer before deciding whether he wanted to continue doing it.

We see too many people try something for a few months, struggle, and then quit saying, "This isn't for me."

But here's the problem: you don't actually know if something isn't for you until you've excelled at it.

If you fail at something and then quit, all you know is that you failed. You don't know if the problem was the activity itself or your approach to it. You don't know if you would have loved it once you got good at it.

So Robert created a rule for himself: he would master something before deciding whether to keep doing it.

When he got into sales, he studied everything he could about influence, persuasion, psychology, and communication. He practiced constantly. He tracked his results. He refined his approach.

And then, at the pinnacle of his success—six months of perfect closes, money pouring in, peak performance—he made a decision.

He didn't like sales.

He understood sales inside and out, but he realized he didn't want to do it the rest of his life.

But he only knew that because he had reached the top first. If he had quit after struggling for a few months, he would always wonder if he had given up too soon.

So our advice to you: if you're going to try something, commit to excellence. Reach the top. Then decide if you want to stay there.

DIG DEEP INTO DISC

The book that really drove this skill home for Robert was *Have a New You By Friday*, by Dr. Kevin Leman.

He explains all of the 4 personality types as dog breeds. For reference, the personality types are:

1. Dominant (D)
2. Influent (I)
3. Stable (S)
4. Conscious (C)

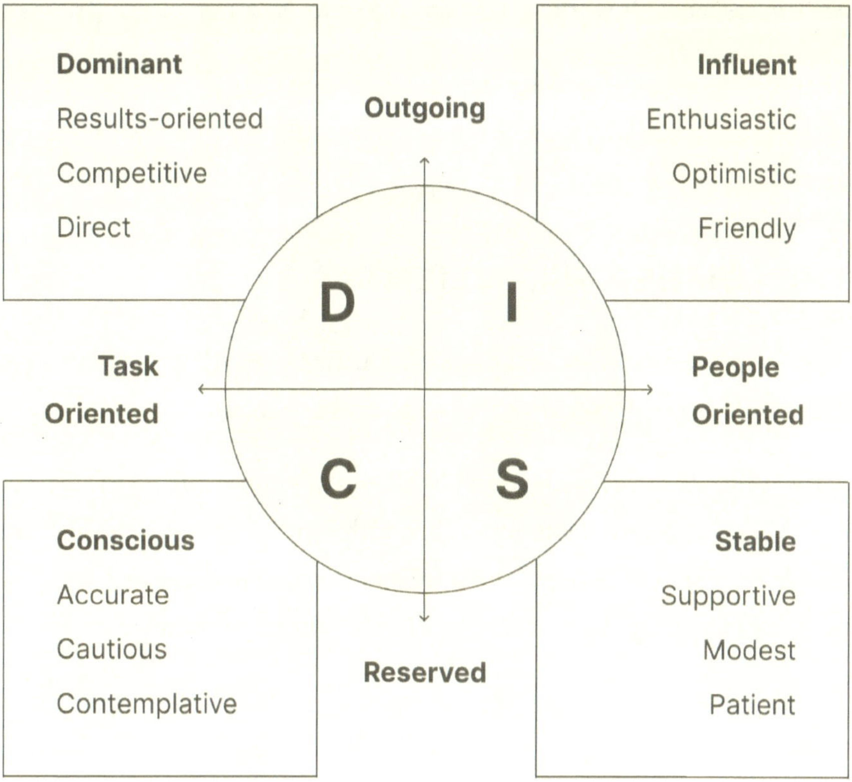

Graphic: DISC Personalities Diagram.

Dominants are represented as Great Danes, Influents as Yorkshire Terriers, and so on.

It's one of the funniest non-fiction books we've ever read!

At one point he explains how one of his uncles, a poodle, and an aunt, a great dane, were arguing about how to paint a wall, or something like that. We can't remember the exact story, but Robert remembers crying with laughter as he was recalling their dialog, considering NEITHER of them knew anything about painting walls!!

After reading that book, for months Robert looked at people and thought "Oh... they're a poodle... OK, this is how I need to speak and act to get along with them."

And, guess what? It worked. 100% of the time. Not a single exception.

This is incredibly powerful, but we don't want to make this book 2,000 pages long. Hence why we very openly share with you where we've learned everything, so if you want to go deeper, you can.

THE LUMBER MILL CLIENT

Patrick has a similar story that perfectly illustrates what happens when you don't understand personality types—and what happens when you do.

Early in Patrick's sales career, he had a client at a lumber mill on the Oregon coast. The guy behaved like a total jerk with him. He was always short and dismissive. He never wanted to chat. Never wanted to talk about anything personal like his family or interests, like the other clients did.

Patrick kept trying to build rapport the way he'd been taught: be friendly, find common ground, show interest in their life. But every time he tried, the client would cut him off. "Did you get the boiler results? What about the test? Okay, thanks, bye."

Patrick was about to lose an $80,000 deal with the client because he was putting the project out to bid with competitors.

Then Patrick attended DISC training.

He suddenly realized: this guy wasn't a jerk. He was a high D (Dominant). He didn't want small talk. He didn't want Patrick wasting his time. He just wanted results, delivered efficiently.

The next time Patrick visited the client, he completely changed his approach. He walked in, gave the client the results. He was short with him, and then he left. No chitchat. No rapport-building. Just the information the client needed, delivered quickly.

The *next* visit, *the client* started talking to Patrick about fishing and suggested possibly going out on his boat together!

Why? Because Patrick finally spoke the client's language. He respected his communication style. He stopped trying to force his own style on the client, and instead started interacting in the way the client preferred.

Patrick saved that $80,000 account, and maintained that relationship for years because he finally understood how to communicate with him.

NEUROLINGUISTIC PROGRAMMING (NLP)

Once you understand DISC, you can layer on another powerful technique: Neurolinguistic Programming, or NLP.

The basic principle is simple: people trust people who are like them.

So you can build rapport faster by subtly mirroring someone's:

- Body language
- Rate of speech
- Tone of voice
- Word choices
- Energy level

This isn't about being fake or manipulative. It's about meeting people where they are.

If someone speaks slowly and thoughtfully, and you speak fast and energetically, there's a disconnect and they are less likely to trust you. But if you slow down and match their pace, they feel more comfortable.

Here's a pro tip: After you've mirrored someone for 10-15 minutes, test your rapport by doing something different. Lean back when they've been leaning forward. Change your pace. If they unconsciously mirror YOU in return, you've built genuine rapport. You're ready to move the conversation forward.

ACTION STEPS

1. Take a free DISC assessment online. Understand your own dominant personality type.

2. Study all four DISC types until you can describe each one without referring to notes.

3. For the next week, consciously identify the personality type of everyone you interact with. Keep a journal of your observations.

4. Choose three people you interact with regularly (boss, colleague, family member) and write down their likely personality types. Then adjust how you communicate with them for one week and note any differences.

5. Read *Have a New You by Friday* by Dr. Kevin Leman for deeper insights into personality dynamics.

6. Practice NLP mirroring in low-stakes conversations. Notice when rapport builds naturally.

For the most up-to-date links to DISC Personality Assessments or other online tools, just follow the link in the Resources section of this book.

CHAPTER 4

MODEL THE MASTERS

Here's a question: Why would you try to figure everything out from scratch when someone else has already solved the problem?

It might sound obvious when we put it that way. But the factual reality is most people spend their entire lives reinventing the wheel.

They struggle with challenges that thousands of others have already conquered. They make mistakes that could have been easily avoided by simply learning from those who came before.

There's a principle that changed everything for us. We first learned it from Tony Robbins, and then later saw Jack Canfield dedicate an entire chapter to it in *The Success Principles*.

The principle is simple: Success leaves clues.

If you want to achieve something—anything—find someone who's already achieved it. Study what they did. Learn their methods. Model their approach. Then add your own spin if you want..

THE ROMANIAN DESIGN LESSON

When Robert started his engineering company, Wesrom, he was living in Oradea, a city on the border between Hungary and Romania. This was early in his career. He was ambitious but inexperienced.

He knew Wesrom would be an engineering firm that built both hardware and software for clients. But he didn't know exactly how to position the company, or what their work should look like.

So Robert did what the principle teaches: he looked for someone who was already succeeding in this space.

He found a local Romanian company whose work hel'l never forget. They had the most beautiful portfolio he'd ever seen. Stunning websites for big local businesses. Clean design. Perfect aesthetics. Every detail, polished.

Robert was starstruck.

He remembers thinking, "This is amazing. This is what I want to create. This is the direction I want to go in."

And in that moment, Robert learned two critical lessons:

LESSON 1: YOU SAW AN EXAMPLE

Before seeing that portfolio, building world-class websites felt abstract. After seeing it, Robert knew it was possible. He had proof. And once you have proof that something can be done, it becomes infinitely easier to believe you can do it too.

LESSON 2: AESTHETICS MATTER

There were other companies making more money. There were other companies with bigger clients. But this was the company that left an impact. Why? Because their work looked amazing.

Robert realized: he can't be the only person who appreciates beautiful design. If aesthetics matter to a young company founder in Romania, they would matter to clients too.

Interestingly enough, Robert was unaware that Steve Jobs, on the other side of the world, was already championing the importance of aesthetics. His emphasis on design at Apple turned that company into the trillion dollar company it is today.

Robert made the decision that everything Wesrom built would look amazing. Every detail would be polished. Every project would be something they were proud to show.

That single observation—modeling what that company did with design—shaped Wesrom's entire trajectory.

After Robert studied their portfolio and implemented what he learned about design and aesthetics, Wesrom started building. And everything they produced looked amazing.

Then they started attracting amazing clients.

They landed Westpac—the second-largest bank in Australia. They built apps for Stanford University. They landed A+ International Healthcare, who were the largest healthcare insurance policy maker in Hong Kong at the time. They landed a major Romanian tourism leader as a client, and built out their entire infrastructure.

Just look at the geography breadth of their clients: the United States. Australia. Asia. Europe. Wesrom was working with billion-dollar brands across four continents!

They made millions of dollars doing this work, and made tens of millions for their clients.

But here's the twist in the story.

Over ten years after Robert first discovered that local company in Oradea—his north star, the company he looked up to and modeled, when he moved back to Oradea, he was walking through local streets, being hit by waves of nostalgia. And he remembered them.

So he looked them up.

The company doesn't exist anymore. We don't know if they went bankrupt or just closed down. But this company that was once Robert's shining jewel, his north star—they're gone.

And in those same ten years, Robert delivered on more projects and has made far more revenue than they ever did. (Robert actually looked up their records)

Why?

Because they knew how to serve small companies in a small city. Oradea had less than a quarter million people. Small companies, small budgets, small projects worth tens of thousands of dollars.

But Robert took what they (indirectly) taught him about design and excellence, and applied it to a bigger vision. They went after billion-dollar brands with six- and seven-figure budgets.

You can do the same. Learn whatever you need to learn from others, and then carve your own path through life.

DON'T TAKE HEALTH ADVICE FROM...

Here's a principle we tell people all the time. It's a profound truth wrapped up in a joke:

Don't take health advice from someone who's overweight.

Don't take relationship advice from someone who's single (unless they're old and widowed, obviously).

Don't take financial advice from someone who's broke.

Don't take business advice from someone who's never built a successful business.

If you want to learn something, find someone who's actually achieved the result you want. Not someone who talks about it. Not someone who read about it. Someone who did it.

This seems obvious, but you'd be shocked how often people ignore this principle.

They take fitness advice from their out-of-shape friend.

They take investment advice from their broke uncle.

They take business advice from people who've never run a highly-profitable business.

And then they wonder why they're not getting results...

Don't be that person. Instead, put in the effort to find the people who have achieved the results you want. Learn from them. Model what they do.

SHADOWING A MASTER SALESMAN

Patrick has a perfect example of this principle in action.

When Patrick first got into B2B sales with a twenty-billion-dollar company, he had no idea what he was doing. He was enthusiastic and willing to learn, but he was starting from zero.

So he did the smartest thing he could have done: he shadowed his boss.

Every single sales call he could attend, he was there. He watched. Took notes on everything. Every objection his boss encountered, Patrick would write down his response word-for-word. Every technique he used, Patrick documented it.

For two months, he was a sponge. He absorbed everything.

Then when he started making his own sales calls, he essentially became his boss. He used his boss's language. He copied his tonality. He mirrored his authority. Patrick practiced in front of a mirror until he could deliver his responses with the same confidence his boss had.

In Patrick's second year as a sales executive, he became the number one sales rep for the District. That's almost unheard of for someone so new. But it wasn't magic. He just modeled someone who was already excellent at what he was trying to learn.

THE CIRCLE OF LIFE

Here's something important to remember: No master stays a master forever.

Everyone eventually passes the baton to someone else. That's just the circle of life. (If you need to learn about the circle of life, just watch The Lion King. Seriously. Great movie. Timeless wisdom).

Muhammad Ali was the best boxer in the world. Then Mike Tyson became the greatest. Then someone else.

Each generation learns from the previous one and adds their own innovations. The masters teach the students, and eventually the students become the new masters.

Your job isn't to worship the masters from afar. Your job is to learn from them, implement their lessons, improve on their methods, and eventually become a master yourself.

And then you pass it on to the next generation.

That's how progress happens.

ACTION STEPS

1. List three specific goals you want to achieve in the next 12 months. Be precise.

2. For each goal, identify 2-3 people who have already achieved that result. Write down their names.

3. Choose ONE goal and ONE master to focus on for the next 30 days.

4. Create a learning plan: What books will you read? What courses will you take? What content will you consume?

5. Schedule 30 minutes daily for the next 30 days to study your chosen master.

6. Either during or at the end of the 30 days, implement at least three principles you learned. Track your results.

For the most up-to-date list of books we recommend, just follow the link in the Resources section of this book.

CHAPTER 5

START HOW SESSIONS

Everyone talks about journaling these days. The benefits of reflection, of putting pen to paper, of tracking your thoughts and progress. We like the idea. We really do.

There's something profound about self-reflection. Someone far wiser than us once said that if everyone would just reflect on their own actions and words, we wouldn't have wars. The world would be a much better place. We've journaled for many years, and we genuinely believe in the practice.

But we also like to be practical. Very practical.

And that's where How Sessions changed everything for us.

LEARNING FROM A BILLIONAIRE

We discovered How Sessions through Patrick Grove. You might not know his name, but you should. Patrick is a friend of Vishen Lakhiani, founder of Mindvalley. A few years ago, Vishen invited Patrick to speak at one of his events in Bali and interviewed him on stage.

Patrick Grove was born a normal guy. Just like you and me. Sure, he had a crazy work ethic—like all self-made billionaires do. But the main thing he attributes his success to isn't hustle or luck or connections.

It's How Sessions.

After watching that interview, Robert had the pleasure of talking with

Patrick several times. He'd already become a billionaire. Robert dove deeper into his methodology and how he uses it. What Robert learned completely transformed how he approached challenges, goals, and growth.

WHAT'S A HOW SESSION?

A How Session is deceptively simple. You ask one question that starts with the word "How."

How can I make half a million dollars in the next year?

How can I lose 38 pounds in the next six months?

How can I double my business revenue while maintaining profit margins?

You write that question at the top of a blank page. Then you write 20 answers. And you do not stop until you have all 20 answers to that one question.

Once you have all 20, and no less than 20 answers, then you pick one, or a combination of a few of them, that will get you the outcome you want in the fastest possible way.

That's it. That's the entire system.

But here's what makes it powerful: You'll find that the first five or ten answers come very quickly and very obviously. These are the surface-level solutions you already know about. The "common sense" answers.

Then it starts becoming difficult.

And that's exactly where the magic happens.

After those first easy answers, your creative juices kick in. Your mind must come up with alternative solutions beyond what is normal, common, or conventional. At this point, you're giving your real life challenge the attention it deserves.

The moment you give it that level of attention, you open up channels in your brain that need to be opened. You unlock solutions that were sitting there all along, waiting for you to dig just a little deeper.

WHEN WE USE HOW SESSIONS

We've used How Sessions in multiple scenarios over the years. We've used them when everything was going perfectly. For example, how to accelerate whatever goal we're working on at the time.

We've used them during the darkest periods of our business lives—when nothing was working and we felt completely stuck.

Good days or bad days, How Sessions work.

BREAKING THROUGH MENTAL LOOPS

Here's the problem many ambitious people face: mental loops.

You do things. You're posting on Facebook. You're sending the emails. You're making the calls. But nothing's happening.

You ask yourself: What else should I do? What am I not doing well? What am I missing?

And you go into these mental loops that don't allow you to progress.

But when you have a How Session... you break the loop.

Let's say your challenge is that you're sending emails and nobody is replying. If you do a How Session on "How can I get more people to reply to my emails?", here's what might come out:

- Study what the best subject lines are to increase open rates
- See if there are ways to improve deliverability so more of our emails avoid the spam box
- Test with both long- and short-form emails, see which one gets more replies
- Test different levels and types of humor. Maybe even mention things that have nothing to do with the subject, like "I decided to wear pink socks today. Just FYI."

And on and on, until you get twenty answers. Some obvious. Some creative. Some you might have never thought of without forcing yourself to get to 20.

Even if you implement just a few of those, you're taking action in the direction of your goals. That's what How Sessions do—they give you clarity on what the next steps need to be.

HOW SESSIONS IN CLIENT WORK

We've used How Sessions many, many times within our businesses and within our Partners' businesses. Many of our partners have been working at their businesses for 10, sometimes 20 years, and haven't been able to get to where they wanted to go.

When we come in, many times it's a mess. A very, very big mess. They don't have what they need in the business. Some things are lacking completely. Other things are there, but they're malfunctioning. They're not optimized. People don't know what they should be doing. There's no cohesive alignment with the vision or goals of the business.

Now, because we, the team behind Elkridge Advisors, have done this so many times, we just have a very good gut feeling of what needs to be done. And we tend to move very quickly.

However, when someone has been working in a business for 20 years and hasn't grown it, you can imagine that we need to put in a lot of very specialized thought.

How Sessions help us tremendously.

If you sit down and ask: "How can we increase profitability by 100%?" For a business that has already tried to increase their profit margin for the last five years and failed, that's not an easy task.

But you sit down. You do a How Session. You come up with 20 ways you can increase profits. Then you start implementing the lowest hanging fruit immediately.

After you implement those and have some success, you can either continue with the first list from the How Session, or you can do another session. Often, new insights come the second time around.

And guess what? Implement enough of those 20 answers, and profits increase. Every time. Like clockwork.

NOT MEDITATION. NOT LEARNING.

With How Sessions, you're literally doing deep work for however long it takes you to get 20 answers.

Sometimes people ask me: "When do I do a How Session versus just looking things up online or taking a course?"

Great question.

Many times, some of the points in your How Session will be about learning what to do. Because sometimes you just don't know. Let's say you don't know how to improve an ad campaign. So you take a course on ads. Or you don't know how to improve your closing rate on a sales call. One of your How Session answers might be: "Review a recording of a previous call and see what I can do better." Another might be: "Read a book on how to close more effectively."

The How Session itself can include educational steps. Not all 20 answers will be, but some of them might be. That's perfectly fine.

ACTION STEPS

Do at least one How Session this week.

Pick something specific that matters to you right now. Not "How can I be more successful?" but something concrete:

- How can I make $X in the next Y months?
- How can I improve my relationship with my spouse?
- How can I get my next three clients?

Here's the process:

1. Write your "How" question at the top of a blank page
2. Force yourself to write 20 answers (not 15, not 18—minimum 20)
3. Push through the discomfort when it gets difficult
4. Review all 20 answers and circle the top 3 most actionable with

highest likelihood of success

5. Start implementing immediately

The first ten will come easily. The discomfort you feel writing the next ten is exactly where the breakthrough happens. That's where your brain opens up new channels and finds solutions that have been hiding in plain sight.

Don't skip this. Do it today.

This one practice can unlock more progress than months of spinning your wheels in mental loops.

CHAPTER 6

PRIORITIZE EVERYTHING

It seems too simple.

That's what they said back then. And that's what you'll probably think after learning the strategy we use to prioritize.

But this simple system made us millions. And it can do the same for you.

Over the past 15 years we've learned about and experimented with dozens of productivity and time management strategies, one of which has stood the test of time as the most effective of them all.

This is the exact same strategy Charles M Schwab and his executives at Bethlehem Steel used to build an empire which employed over 300,000 people and became the second largest steel manufacturer in the US.

Now, it might be important to note we don't admire many of Charles's other habits, but very few teams are as effective with their time as to build a billion dollar company in just a couple decades.

There were many other capable steel manufacturers around. How were they able to get done so much more and grow so much faster than everyone else?

It's a little strategy called...

THE IVY LEE METHOD

Ivy Ledbetter Lee was one of the pioneers of public relations, highly-respected for his productivity. He even worked with the late John D. Rockefeller himself.

In 1918, Charles arranged to meet with Ivy and asked him if he could help him and his team "get more things done."

Ivy said he can, and that he just needs to spend 15 minutes with each of Charles' executives.

Charles, surprised, asked how much would he charge for those 2-3 hours of work?

Ivy then famously said: "Nothing."

After a brief pause, he continued to explain that he should be paid only if the strategy actually works.

And if it does, in three months, Charles can send him a check for whatever he and the team feel it's worth.

Three months later, Charles wrote Ivy a check worth the equivalent of over $200,000 today... almost a quarter million dollars...

This was the value Charles and his team attributed to this one productivity and time management strategy.

Now, we know this was quite a long ramp-up, but this strategy is so incredibly simple that we did not want you doubting its effectiveness.

Here it is:

At the end of each day, write down the six most important things you want to get done tomorrow, prioritized in order of their true importance.

You must decide which of these six priorities is the top one most important. Then which one's number two, and so on.

As a note, we all feel we have more than six things to do in a given day, but please do not allow yourself to have more than six. This is part of the strategy.

Then, the moment you start working tomorrow, you start by working on your number one priority, and you don't allow yourself to do anything else until that top one priority is done.

Only when done do you allow yourself to go to number two on your list. (Which now should be your top priority from the list).

If you don't finish everything on your list, at the end of the day you assess whether the remaining items should be on your top priority list for tomorrow, or decide if some new priorities that came up during the day will require writing a completely new list of six for tomorrow.

That's it.

Try this every single day for a couple weeks, and you'll be amazed at how effective it is.

After over a decade in business, we have a pretty good sense of what is the most important task we can do to keep growing revenue and profits every year, so the most critical step of the entire process is not allowing ourselves to work on anything else until we've finished our top priority.

Those are the two aspects we feel this entire strategy boils down to. One, have the wisdom to decide what is truly the most important thing we should be doing right now. Two, doon't allow yourself to do anything else than that one thing.

Why would Schwab pay that much for such simple advice? Because he recognized a profound truth: most people fail not because they don't know what to do, but because they don't prioritize what matters most.

TIME: THE GREAT EQUALIZER

All of us have the same 24 hours in a day.

Think about it. Look at Patrick Grove—the billionaire we mentioned in the last chapter. Then look at both of us: Patrick Rogers, and Robert Indries. Then look at yourself.

Patrick Grove is already a billionaire. The rest of us aren't. Yet.

What's the difference? We all had roughly the same amount of time pass. Grove is about 50 years old. Similar timeline. Some of us were born in different countries, sure. But time passes the same for everyone.

The only difference—the *only* difference—is how we prioritize our time.

Again, time passes the same for everyone. The only difference in effectiveness between two people is what they prioritize.

If your priorities are straight, if you always work on your number one priority, you will achieve so much more in life than you would have ever imagined.

ACTIONS, NOT GOALS

We need to clarify something important. There's a difference between goals and tasks. The list method focuses on *actions* that you take.

You might be thinking: "I can have a list of top six priorities for the year, for the quarter, for the month."

Hold on. What you're describing are overarching goals or objectives. Let's say your objective is to make $100,000 in revenue this year. That's a goal. That's a *lag measure*—an outcome that only happens after you take action.

To reach that lag measure, you need *lead measures*—the actual action steps you take. Those are numbered one through six on your daily list.

The list method isn't about setting goals. It's about taking action on the specific tasks that move you toward those goals.

THE DEEP WORK ADVANTAGE

This system forces you to do deep work all the time.

You have five pending tasks and one main task. You don't touch the five. You just have them there, written down, so you have a little plan. But you work on the first one. Just the first one. Until it's done.

If you keep doing this, it's incredible how much more productive you are than almost everyone else on the planet.

WHAT ABOUT EVERYTHING ELSE?

You might be thinking. "What about the daily things I have to do just to maintain life and business? What about eating, showering, taking the kids to school? If my priority is working out to build muscle, does that mean I skip everything else?"

Let's be clear. We've gone many days without eating either breakfast, lunch, or dinner, or either. Today, Robert's first meal was at 3 PM because he was busy all day. Eating wasn't the priority until 3 PM when he was "starving."

Whatever you need to skip to get your number one highest priority done, you skip.

If you're hemorrhaging money, if you really need cash flow, you will very quickly skip everything that doesn't generate revenue. It's crazy how quickly and how effectively you will stop doing things that aren't bringing in or keeping paying clients. You will only work on revenue-generating activities because that's your lifeblood.

When life is good and comfortable, you give yourself permission to be mediocre. But when you're forced to focus—when you have to—you prioritize ruthlessly.

The list method is a self-forcing mechanism. It makes you prioritize even when you don't have to. You prioritize because you should. Because it's better for you.

Now, let's be clear about this as well: mature adults don't neglect things. You don't neglect your responsibilities. You prioritize.

If today your priority is a client presentation and you don't have time to work out, you work on that presentation. Tomorrow you work out. You're not neglecting fitness—you're prioritizing what matters most right now.

If taking your kids to school is non-negotiable, that stays. But maybe sleep becomes flexible. Robert regularly sleeps four hours at night because he wakes up excited about something at 4 AM. Then he works for a few hours and takes a nap at 10 AM. Sleep is still a priority—he just arranges it differently based on what matters most in the moment.

THE 12 WEEK YEAR

The 12 Week Year by Brian P. Moran is a concept that plays in the same bucket as the list method.

The whole idea behind The 12 Week Year is collapsing time. Instead of thinking in annual terms, you think in "12-week years." When you do this correctly, you can accomplish in three months what most people accomplish in a year or longer.

Here's why this matters: Without prioritization, you won't make real progress.

The 12 Week Year creates KPIs around your commitment to action. Not vague goals, but specific action items you commit to each week.

Let's say you have 10 action items for the week. If you accomplish at least 70% of those action items each week, you'll hit your quarterly goals. That's the threshold. Seventy percent completion.

This puts accountability behind those action items. And as we said earlier, you can't measure lag measures and expect to accomplish your goals. If you only measure lag measures, it's already too late. You have to measure your lead measures—the actions you're actually taking. That's how we accomplish things in life.

ACTION STEPS

This week, implement the Ivy Lee Method.

Here's exactly what to do:

1. **Lay out your plan for the next 12 weeks.** What are the 100 or however many items you want to achieve during this period? Spread those across the 12 weeks. This does not need to be perfect. This just needs to give you direction. It shouldn't take more than 1-2 hours to do.

2. **At the end of each workday, write down your top six priorities for tomorrow.** Rank them in order of importance.

3. **The next morning, start working on priority number one.** Do not touch priorities two through six until priority one is complete.

4. **When priority one is done, check your list.** Does the order need to change? Did something urgent come up? Adjust if needed. Then work on your new number one priority.

5. **Repeat this process every single day for one week.**

Do this for seven days. Just seven days. (The equivalent of 1 month, in the 12-Week year system)

You'll be shocked at how much more you accomplish compared to almost any other approach.

The system seems too simple. That's why it works. Complexity is the enemy of execution. Simplicity is your competitive advantage.

CHAPTER 7

MANAGE YOUR LIFE ENERGY

Interestingly enough, most people have personal or professional development completely backward.

When they start a self-improvement journey, what do they do? They add things. They add 10 minutes of journaling. They add 30 minutes of meditation. They add running or gym time. They add making their bed every morning. They keep adding and adding and adding.

That's their version of self-improvement—piling more activities onto an already overloaded life.

We believe in the exact opposite. The main way to achieve more in life is through subtraction. Through the strategic removal of the useless. Through the elimination of distractions.

To say it more plainly: You don't need more time. You just need less distractions.

You don't need to eat more healthy food. You just need to stop eating unhealthy food.

It's about subtraction, not addition. The more non-essential things you can remove from your life, the better.

WARREN BUFFET'S 25/5 RULE

Do you know the story about Warren Buffett's personal airplane pilot, Mike Flint?

Flint flew for Buffett for ten years. Before that, he'd flown four US Presidents. So we can safely say he's exceptional at what he does—the kind of person who operates at the highest levels.

One day, Flint was talking with Buffett about his career priorities. Buffett saw an opportunity to teach him something valuable.

"Mike," Buffett said, "let's do an exercise. Write down your top 25 career goals."

Flint took some time and wrote them down. Twenty-five things he wanted to accomplish in his career.

Important Note: If you want to do this exercise right now, stop reading here. Write down your 25 goals before continuing. Don't read further until you've written them down.

When he finished, Buffett gave him the second instruction: "Now review your list and circle your top 5 goals. Just five."

Flint went through his list carefully. He thought about what mattered most. Eventually, he circled five goals—the ones that were most important to him.

Now Flint had two lists. List A: the 5 items he had circled. List B: the 20 items he hadn't circled.

Flint looked at his List A and said, "Okay, I'll start working on these top 5 goals right away."

Buffett nodded. Then he asked about the other list: "And what about the ones you didn't circle?"

Flint replied, "Well, the top 5 are my primary focus, but the other 20 come in a close second. They're still important, so I'll work on those as I see fit. They're not as urgent, but I still plan to give them dedicated effort."

Buffett shook his head.

"No. You've got it wrong, Mike."

He pointed at List B—the 20 items Flint hadn't circled.

"Everything you didn't circle just became your Avoid-At-All-Cost list. No matter what, these things get no attention from you until you've succeeded with your top 5."

ROBERT'S FOUR PRIORITIES

Buffett was actually generous when he said five. Some people say you should have only one priority. In the book *The One Thing*, authors Gary Keller and Jay Papasan advocate extreme focus on just one thing.

For Robert, as a parent, that doesn't work. He has a business, but he also has children. And Robert believes he can't take care of his children and his business without taking care of his health.

So he sets four priorities. They're the roles Robert has chosen for himself as a man and as a person:

1. **Provider** - Financial, career, generating income for his family

2. **Family Man** - Husband, father, son

3. **Health** - Making sure he's healthy. Healthy food, workouts.

4. **Education** - Robert loves reading, learning, evolving

That's it. These are his only four priorities. Anything else he just avoids.

If a friend says "Hey, can you hang out this weekend?", he can spend a couple hours with them. But friendship is not in his "Top 5 priorities." If Robert's wife says, "Let's go visit my parents," they go visit her parents. Because Robert's priorities are crystal clear.

Robert has these four, and they never compete with one another because there's always time for all four. Why? Because Robert has only set four. Not twelve. Four.

He has strategically subtracted everything else from his life. He doesn't have any other goals besides doing these four things well. In the future, he might have other goals in other areas of his life. But for now, there's only these four.

We have a finite level of energy every single day. If you're dispersed on too many things, you'll be mediocre at all of them. But if you focus on just a few things—one to four—you can do those well to a high enough level of quality that you'll be happy with your accomplishments in all of them.

Everything else is a distraction.

THE POWER OF NO

Here's what happens when you get serious about your priorities: You have to start saying no.

Patrick and Robert have both struggled with this. We're both natural people-pleasers. We might do two or three times the effort for someone else than for ourselves.

But you must prioritize. The moment you prioritize and define your top four or five, that's it. You don't have anything else.

You might upset some people. You might hurt some relationships. Some friendships might fade. But to achieve your goals, you must prioritize your time. Sometimes that means saying no to things you used to love to do before.

Stop being a people pleaser if you want to achieve your goals. It's that simple.

For example: We have family on our lists. We can go to the cinema to watch a movie with our families. We can watch a series together. But watching Netflix isn't a waste of time *if it falls within one of your categories.*

For Robert, watching movies isn't a priority. But his wife Diana loves watching movies. So every week they watch at least one. That's 50+ movies a year. That's a lot by many people's standards. But that's fine because it falls within Robert's "Family Man" priority.

THE CAPTURE LIST

As an ambitious person, you don't know all 1,000 steps you need to take. Right now, you might know the next 10 steps. So you write those down. You choose your top six priorities. Then you start working on priority number one.

While you're working, you get ideas. "Oh, I should also do X. I need to follow up with Y. Someone asked me to do Z."

Here's what most people do: They stop what they're doing and chase these thoughts. They go to their inbox to send that email. While they're there, they see another email that just came in. They reply to that one too. Then they go down a rabbit hole of reactive work. They forget what they were originally doing. It takes them a few seconds to remember. They work for a few minutes. Then they remember something else they need to do. The cycle repeats.

They get nothing meaningful done. Or at least way less than they would have if they would have focused.

Here's what we do instead: we keep a capture list.

Every single thought that pops into your head—every task, every idea, every reminder—goes on the capture list. All of them. Everything.

Then it's off your mind. It's on the capture list. That's it.

We cannot tell you how much mental energy and bandwidth this gives you. It's insane.

You add it to the capture list. You stop thinking about it. You refocus on whatever you need to do.

When you finish a top priority, you might look at your capture list. It might have five items on it. You can look at it and think: "Can I just knock these out in the next 25 minutes?" Many times you can. Just do a quick Pomodoro session—set a timer for 25 minutes—and get those done.

Then you move on to priority number two.

If the capture list items aren't that important, they can wait. If your spouse asks you to change a light bulb. put it on the capture list and make it a priority later—maybe that evening, maybe tomorrow. That way it won't derail your most important work.

The capture list is your safety net. It ensures nothing falls through the cracks while protecting your focus on what matters most.

And now that we've talked the mind, let's wrap up with...

MOVE YOUR BODY

We exude more energy the healthier we are. If we're sedentary all the time, our life energy goes down.

You should build some form of movement or muscle building into your schedule. Whether that's going to the gym, doing bodyweight workouts, or playing a physical game.

Robert and his wife play tennis from time to time. It's really enjoyable. Sometimes Robert plays basketball with friends. Patrick works out almost every day with HIIT and weights—lots of movement, lots of physical activity.

If you don't intentionally move in this day and age, you will probably find that you move less than your body should.

We won't turn this into a health book. There are many books on health, and this won't be one of them. But physical movement directly impacts your mental energy and your ability to execute on your priorities.

ACTION STEPS

This week, conduct your personal energy audit.

1. **Do the Warren Buffett 25/5 exercise.** Write down 25 goals or things you want to achieve. Then circle your top 5. Those other 20? You avoid them with all your might until your top 5 are complete.

2. **Define your 3-6 priorities.** What are the roles or areas of life that matter most to you? Write them down clearly. Everything outside these priorities is a distraction.

3. **Identify ONE energy drain.** Find one thing—just one—that's an energy drain or a life drain. It could be:

    - A toxic relationship
    - Binge-watching too many series
    - Doom scrolling on social media
    - Playing excessive video games
    - A commitment you made out of guilt
    - Whatever is draining your life energy

4. **Remove it from your life.** You don't even need to remove it completely if you're dependent on it (like an addiction). But remove as much of it as you can. Start this week.

5. **Practice saying "No" three times this week.** When someone asks you to do something that doesn't align with your priorities,

practice saying: "I appreciate you thinking of me, but I can't commit to that right now." No explanation needed. No guilt either.

6. **Start a capture list today.** Keep it in a note on your phone, a notebook, or wherever is most convenient. Every time a thought or task pops into your head while you're working on your top priority, immediately add it to the capture list. Don't think about it. Don't act on it. Just capture it and refocus.

7. **At the end of each day, review your capture list.** Decide which items need to become priorities for tomorrow and which can wait.

8. **Schedule movement.** Put physical activity on your calendar at least three times this week. Make it non-negotiable. It could be 20 minutes—just move your body intentionally.

The path to achieving more isn't adding more. It's removing what doesn't matter so you can focus fully on what does.

Energy is life. Life is energy. Manage yours wisely and enjoy the benefits.

CHAPTER 8

NETWORK BETTER

There's a book you should know about: *Who Not How* by Benjamin Hardy and Dan Sullivan.

The core principle is simple but powerful: It's way easier to find someone who can help you do what you need to do than to try to do everything yourself.

In business and in life, you can decide to do everything yourself. But many times, it's much easier—and much more effective—if you have other people help you.

This chapter isn't just about networking. It's about understanding that the people you surround yourself with will fundamentally shape your financial future.

THE TOP 5 PEOPLE IN YOUR LIFE

You probably already know this, but it's so important, it warrants at least a couple paragraphs as a reminder. Because all of us are too prone to falling into comfortable habits and relationships. Whomever you surround yourself with, you unconsciously imitate to some extent. Their beliefs influence yours. You subconsciously absorb some of their attitudes. You maybe even mirror some of their habits.

It's unavoidable. The human brain is wired for social learning and mimicry.

It's far easier to just surround yourself with people who push you forward. And if you're serious about building wealth, you need to take this seriously.

Look at the five people you spend the most time with—the people you *choose* to invest your time with. What are their financial habits? What's their average net worth? What's their average income?

That average is very likely close to where you are right now. And if you want to be somewhere different five years from now, it will help to change who you're spending time with.

READ IF YOU DON'T HAVE RICH FRIENDS

Here's the good news: If you don't currently know five wealthier, more successful people you can spend time with, you can start with reading.

Reading is like having a direct conversation with the author. You can sit down with the Stoics. You can have your morning tea with Napoleon Hill. You can absorb wisdom from Peter Drucker, Jack Canfield, or any other successful person who's written a book.

Those are real conversations that can shape your thinking, your beliefs, and your actions.

Surround yourself with books written by the top five people whose success you want to emulate. It's similar to modeling the masters, but in this case, you're starting with reading. Then you can connect with successful people in person later.

PATRICK AND ROBERT'S PARTNERSHIP

Here's a real-world example: our partnership (Patrick and Robert's).

We have similar backgrounds. We've both succeeded at engineering, running businesses, consulting, and M&A. We have a lot of common ground.

At the same time, we have very different preferences for *how* we work.

Patrick is much more extroverted than Robert. He loves talking to people. He loves meeting people. He genuinely enjoys sales and the continuity of relationships. He's energized by being the face of the company.

Robert is the opposite. He's much more introverted. He likes building things in the back. He doesn't care if no one knows his name. He really doesn't want to be visible. He just likes building stuff.

When we met and joined forces, it meant that both of us could achieve much more because we're together in this partnership.

Could Robert do sales? Absolutely. He's closed tens of millions of dollars in sales throughout his career. But Patrick is better at it than Robert is, and more importantly, he *loves* it. So we chose for him to be in charge of revenue and client relationships.

Robert is in charge of the operations side. He's responsible for getting more lead flow to our clients, for making sure there's follow-through on every lead, for building systems that work.

Neither side is easy. But both of us are much happier doing our side than we would be if we had to do all sides ourselves.

This is an amazing case study of the "Who Not How" principle in action.

We didn't try to become experts at everything. We found someone whose strengths complemented our weaknesses, and whose weaknesses were our strengths.

That's what good networking does. It connects you with people who multiply your effectiveness.

BE INTENTIONAL

Don't spray and pray. Be very conscious and very picky with the people you spend time with.

When we say "picky," we don't mean to offend anybody. But you should be strategic about who gets your time and energy.

Not everyone deserves access to you. Your time is your most valuable asset. Your attention is limited. Your energy is finite.

So be intentional about who you're giving it to.

WHY THIS MATTERS

Neither of us would be where we are today without the people we've had the privilege of working with, learning from, and partnering with.

It doesn't matter if you're an introvert or an extrovert. Robert is an introvert. Patrick is an extrovert. Both of us keep growing the strength of our network every month, if not every week.

Here's why networking is in the top 10 principles for building wealth:

Your network determines your opportunities. The people you know open doors. They introduce you to deals. They share insights. They warn you about mistakes. They provide capital. They become partners. They refer clients.

Without a strong network, you're building wealth with one hand tied behind your back.

HOW TO NETWORK

Here are practical steps for building your network in ways that actually create wealth:

1. ATTEND EVENTS

Go to conferences, seminars, and meetups in your industry or in industries adjacent to where you want to build wealth. Yes, this costs money and time. But even just one good connection can 10X your investment.

2. USE LINKEDIN STRATEGICALLY

This is a business book, not a general self-help book. So when we talk about networking, we're talking about professional, wealth-building networking. That means LinkedIn, not TikTok.

LinkedIn is where serious professionals connect. Use it intentionally.

3. ADD VALUE FIRST

Don't network by asking what people can do for you. Network by figuring out what you can do for them. Share an article they'd find useful. Make an introduction that helps them. Offer insights from your experience.

When you add value first, people remember you. And when opportunities arise, they think of you.

4. FOLLOW UP CONSISTENTLY

Most people meet someone interesting at an event, connect on LinkedIn, and never talk to them again. Don't be like most people.

Follow up. Send a message. Schedule a call. Build an actual relationship, not just a digital connection.

5. UPSCALE YOUR CIRCLE

Look at your current network. Are they helping you progress toward your wealth goals?

There's nothing wrong with old friendships. You can love those people. You can see them occasionally. But it also helps to upscale your group from time to time.

Seek connections with people who are 10 steps ahead of you. People who've already achieved what you're trying to achieve. Those are the relationships that will pull you forward.

QUALITY OVER QUANTITY

You don't need 10,000 LinkedIn connections. You need maybe 10 to 20 *real* relationships with people who are further along the path you want to walk.

One strong relationship with someone who's built a $10 million business is worth more than 100 superficial connections with people who've never built anything.

ACTION STEPS

This week, start building your wealth-focused network.

1. **Read for wisdom.** If you don't yet have five successful people in your life you can learn from, choose five books by authors whose success you want to model. Buy them. Schedule time to read them.

2. **Send 20 connection requests on LinkedIn.** Identify 20 people you genuinely want to have a conversation with. People who are doing what you want to do. People who are where you want to be. Send them connection requests with a brief, personalized note. Don't pitch. Just connect.

3. **Follow up with 5 existing connections.** Think about five people already in your network who you haven't talked to in a while. People who are doing interesting things. Send them a message. Ask how they're doing. Offer to help with something if you can. Strengthen that relationship.

4. **Sign up for one event in the next 90 days.** Find a conference, seminar, or mastermind group in your industry. Something where successful people will be in attendance. Register for it. Put it on your calendar. Commit to going.

CHAPTER 9

THE #1 PRINCIPLE OF SUCCESS

If you want to build wealth—real, sustainable, generational wealth—there's one principle that matters more than all the others combined.

It's the foundation. Everything else we've talked about in this book builds on top of this single principle. Without it, nothing else works. With it, everything becomes possible.

The principle comes from Jack Canfield's book *The Success Principles*. It's principle number one. The most important one:

Take 100% responsibility for your life.

Not 50%. Not 99%. One hundred percent.

TWO DRIVERS IN L.A. TRAFFIC

Jack Canfield tells a story that illustrates this perfectly. It's a story that can help you whenever you want to apply this principle.

Two drivers are stuck in Los Angeles traffic. A reporter interviews both of them, and asks how they feel about the situation.

The first driver complains. They're angry. Frustrated. They blame the city, the other drivers, the construction crews. Nothing is their fault. They're a victim of circumstances.

The second driver has a completely different perspective. They say: "Well, I know there's a high chance of traffic in LA. So I always come prepared with audiobooks and extra snacks. I can do a little bit of work from here on my phone. I also use the time to prepare for my next meeting."

Same traffic. Same situation. Polar opposite attitudes and outcomes.

The difference?

One of them takes 100% responsibility for their life and for everything that happens within it.

THE EGO PROBLEM

Here's what we've noticed: Our ego doesn't allow us to take responsibility for the bad things that happen to us.

You'll notice that typically, people who point fingers or blame others have an issue with ego. They think highly of themselves. They can't accept that they might be responsible for their failures.

Christianity tells us to stay humble. Buddhism teaches us to let go of ego. The Stoics wrote extensively about controlling what we can control and accepting what we can't.

The moment we go against these universal rules—in this case, humility—we will suffer in one way or another. That's what we both believe from our own experiences.

It's very difficult to fight against the ego. We get that. We've both struggled with this.

Here's what Robert started doing, maybe 10 or 15 years ago when he first read *The Success Principles*:

Either fix a problem, or accept a problem. But don't complain about the problem.

Fix it or accept it. Don't complain about it.

For example, Patrick noticed that the number of leads we got this week was less than the number we got last week. We could complain about it. We could look into it and fix it. Or we could accept that there's nothing we can do about it.

But complaining does nothing.

Everything is just information. Everything is just feedback. Nothing is inherently good or bad—it's all data that tells us what's working and what's not.

So you go in and do whatever you can. There might be a solution. There might not be. If there's no solution with our current approach, we can do something else. Different campaigns. Different creative. Different strategy.

But we make changes to fix the problem. We take 100% responsibility for the outcome.

100%, NOT 50%/50%

Here's a story that really drives this home.

Robert was on a coaching call with a client. Many times, even when doing executive business coaching, we end up talking about personal matters. Because our personal lives affect our business performance whether we like it or not.

In this particular case, Robert's client was explaining that he wasn't having a good relationship with his wife. He went on and on, explaining all the problems, all the friction, all the misunderstandings.

Robert asked him: "In your relationship, what percentage of responsibility do you think you have?"

He said, "Well, it's of course 50/50. Me 50%, her 50%."

Robert replied, "It's not 50/50."

He thought for a moment. "Okay, well maybe it can be more on my side, but still, she needs to take some responsibility too."

Robert said, "No. It's not even 99% you and 1% them. It's 100% you and 0% her. That's how you need to look at your life."

He pushed back. "But Robert, that doesn't make sense."

Robert explained: "This is *your* life. She is one actor in your life's movie. But you are the producer. You're the writer. You're the director. And you're the main actor."

The client told a specific story to prove his point. He said:

"I wanted to surprise her. I came home early. I prepared dinner—a meal I knew she'd love. I lit candles. I put on music. I was ready to surprise her and have a beautiful evening together. Then she arrived home, and something had happened at work that day. She was angry. She was snappy. She didn't care about the food. We ended up having a fight because she didn't appreciate what I did for her. Don't you think she should have taken responsibility for that?"

Robert said, "Yes, she should take 100% responsibility for herself and her side of the relationship. But you need to take 100% responsibility for your side. Let me tell you what would have happened if you had truly taken

100% responsibility for that evening.

"If you had taken 100% responsibility, that means you're 100% loving, 100% understanding, 100% patient, 100% caring. The moment your wife entered the room and you could see she was upset, you would have realized that everything you did—the dinner, the candles, the music—mattered less to her in that moment than being listened to. They mattered less than maybe her just being hugged, or having you there to just let them vent.

"You would have realized that your actions that night needed to change. You would have put the dinner aside. You would have sat down with her. You would have listened. If you had taken 100% responsibility for that evening, I guarantee you wouldn't have had a fight. Because you need two people to have a fight. You can't have a fight alone."

He sat with that for a moment. Then he got it.

Now, we're not saying that everyone in a relationship should stay in the relationship. Sometimes taking 100% responsibility means ending it when it's not the right fit. Sometimes you try to fix it. Sometimes you realize you need to go your separate paths.

But you don't complain. You either change it or you accept it.

And in any case, you take 100% responsibility.

100% RESPONSIBILITY FOR YOUR FINANCES

This principle applies to everything. It's 100% for your health. 100% for your career.

And in the case of this book: 100% for your finances.

If you do not have money saved right now, that is 100% your fault.

It's not the government. It's not your parents. It's not your boss. It's not your clients. It's not the economy. It's not anyone else.

It's 100% you.

You did not do what you had to do until now to have the amount of money you want in your bank account.

And here's the good news: Taking 100% responsibility from now on will allow you to build up that treasure chest, whether that's a quarter million, two million, or twenty million.

You can start now and grow from where you are.

COMPLETE ACCOUNTABILITY

Patrick said it took him his whole life to learn this principle. And honestly, he had to learn it the hard way—multiple times.

When something traumatic happened in his life, his default response was to become a cocoon. He would isolate himself from everybody. He believed he had to figure everything out on his own.

What Patrick figured out in the last five to ten years is that the more he opened up and exposed his problems to people he knows and loves, the faster he found solutions.

But here's what Patrick realized: he always had an excuse.

"My marriage fell apart."

"The economy crashed."

"My mentor led me wrong."

Every single time he got close to real success, something happened. And instead of taking responsibility and learning from it, he blamed somebody else. Then he just moved on to the next thing without actually learning the lesson.

What was the real lesson? If Patrick had complete accountability, he couldn't let himself off the hook to move on to something else. He had to sit with the failure. He had to own it. He had to extract the wisdom from it.

Unfortunately, many times we have to learn things the hard way.

DO YOU RETURN THE SHOPPING CART?

This is a principle that completely transformed Patrick's life. It's a simple question:

Do you return the shopping cart?

It sounds ridiculous. But hear us out.

Our society is full of instant gratification. Somebody has a great business idea. They throw a few stones at it. They don't see results after a few days, and they give up. New Year's resolutions are done by January 10th. February, if they're "ambitious."

We don't do the little things in life every day. And those little things are the tipping points that eventually add up to produce results.

You know the right thing to do is return the shopping cart. But when you do, no one is cheering you on, no one is congratulating you. You do it because you know it is the right thing to do.

It hit Patrick like a ton of bricks when he was 270 pounds. None of his businesses were progressing the way he wanted them to. His relationship with his kids was suffering. He kept telling himself the big lie: "I will do 1, 2, 3 *after* I achieve A, B, C."

"I'll spend time with my kids *after* I build the business. I'll get healthy *after* I close this deal. I'll be present *after* I hit my financial goals," he'd say to himself.

But we never get there. We don't do the little things. We work until 10 or 11 at night. And our relationships fall apart because we didn't take the time to do the little things.

Returning the shopping cart. It's such a small thing. Nobody's watching. Nobody cares. You could leave it in the parking space. Who would know?

But Patrick decided: "I'm going to return the shopping cart. Every single time."

And you know what? Everything changed.

Patrick realized he was never truly successful in business until he started returning the shopping cart. He was never successful in his physical fitness journey, He was never successful in his mental health and mindfulness until he started returning the shopping cart every single time.

The mindset to return the shopping cart every single time carries over into everything in your life. Consistency. Persistence. Doing the right thing every time, even when nobody's watching.

How you do one thing is how you do everything. It's no wonder that when people find success in love, they are also very likely finding success in wealth, health and relationships. It kind of all happens at once.

Many times, people need to mature to a certain age before they get this concept. Getting very comfortable with doing the small, daily actions, with no results and no gratification is paramount.

Patrick never saw real, sustainable success until he committed to doing the small things, every day, when no one was looking or cheering me on.

Now, the question is: Do you return the shopping cart?

ACTION STEPS

This week, transform how you take responsibility for your life.

1. **Identify one thing you complain about or blame others for.** Write it down. Be honest with yourself. What's something you regularly complain about or point fingers at? Your boss? Your spouse? The economy? Your education? Your past? Your lack of time?

2. **Promise yourself you'll never complain about it or point fingers at it again.** Make a commitment right now. From this moment forward, you either fix it, accept it, or move on from it. But you don't complain about that one thing any longer.

3. **Apply the 100% rule to one relationship.** Pick one important relationship in your life—personal or professional. For the next week, take 100% responsibility for your side of that relationship. Don't worry about what they're doing. Focus entirely on what you're doing.

4. **Start returning the shopping cart.** Literally. Every single time you go to a store and use a cart, return it to the proper place. Do it even when it's raining. Do it even when you're tired. Do it even when nobody's watching. Notice how this small act of integrity affects other areas of your life.

5. **Audit your excuses.** Write down every excuse you've used in the past month for why you don't have the financial results you want. Look at that list. Then cross out every excuse and write next to it: "100% my responsibility."

6. **Read *The Success Principles* by Jack Canfield.** Get the book. Read chapter one. Then read the whole thing. This book will change your life if you let it.

Taking 100% responsibility is the most empowering decision you'll ever make. It means you're no longer a victim. You're no longer helpless. You're no longer waiting for someone else to fix whatever part of your life you're struggling with.

You're in control. You're the director of your movie.

And that means you can write whatever ending you want.

CHAPTER 10

REACH $300,000 IN ASSETS

Here's a story that will make this chapter's importance crystal clear.

A couple years ago, a friend of Robert's called him with an opportunity. He had a real estate asset he needed to sell quickly. City center. Prime location. Incredible square footage.

"Robert, I have this building. It's amazing. I need $750,000 for it."

Robert asked where it was located and how big it was. When his friend responded, he immediately thought it sounded way below market value.

"That sounds too cheap," Robert told him. "It sounds like there's something wrong."

He laughed. "No, no. Yes, it is very cheap. It's worth much more. But I just need $750,000 cash quickly. If you can give me $750K, I'll give you the asset."

Robert said he'd think about it.

The next day, Robert went to see the property. The moment he saw it, he knew. This was worth at least $1.5 million. Easily. Prime real estate. Incredible location.

He started making calls immediately. Friends. Banks. "Can I get $750K today? This week? In any reasonably short timeframe?"

He couldn't. He had just spent $500,000 buying other real estate the previous month. He only had maybe $50,000 left in liquid cash. Not enough for a down payment that would make the deal work.

He had to pass on the deal.

Robert called his friend back and said, "I'm sorry. I really appreciate the offer, but I just can't make it work right now."

He understood. Then he started calling mutual friends. Same question: "Do you have $750,000?"

Guess what? None of our friends had $750,000 in cash just sitting there that they could access quickly.

So he listed it online. A couple weeks later, it sold for $1.1 million.

$1.1M... and Robert could have made $350,000 in profit in two weeks. After taxes, maybe $250,000. But still, a quarter million dollars.

If he simply had the cash available.

WHY $300,000 MATTERS

That story illustrates exactly why this chapter exists.

All of the opportunities that we—Patrick and Robert—show our clients, all of the wealth-building strategies we'll teach you in Part Two of this book, require that you have liquid assets. At minimum, a quarter million.

Either cash or stocks you can sell, an IRA or 401k you can borrow against. Real estate equity you can tap into. Something.

If you don't have that much saved, these first ten chapters tell you exactly what you need to do to get there.

And even if you're already past $300,000—even if you're like some of our clients with several million in assets—this first part of the book still matters. Maybe you've never done a How Session. Maybe you haven't defined your five priorities out of 25. Maybe you need to improve how you network or take 100% responsibility.

Every principle we teach in Part One will accelerate your wealth journey, regardless of where you're starting.

And for those starting from zero or close to it, this chapter is your roadmap.

THE ARBITRAGE METHOD

Here's how you can start building wealth even if you have almost nothing right now.

When Patrick's kids were younger, he taught them a principle that Gary Vaynerchuk also talks about: arbitrage. Find opportunities where supply and demand are mismatched, position yourself in the middle, and profit from the difference.

Here's what Patrick and his kids did:

They went to yard sales and tag sales. They'd find items they knew would sell for more online. The people holding yard sales aren't reaching a large audience. They're not selling on eBay or Facebook Marketplace. Demand is limited to whoever drives by their house that Saturday morning.

That means demand is low. Which means prices are low. The chances are very low that someone will run across their yard sale and offer them the true value for whatever it is. But, what if you take that and list it online. Boom! Now you can easily reach a lot of people looking for that very thing.

Demand is higher, therefore price will be as well.

They worked on negotiation strategies. They'd find out what something was actually worth online. They'd offer 25% of that value. Negotiate and buy it. Then they'd go online where people were actively looking for that exact item and resell it for twice what they'd paid.

Patrick's kids would make about $300 on their second transaction.

Then they'd do it again. Find something at a yard sale that sells online for $1,000. Pay $500 for it. Sell it for $900. Make a quick $400.

They just kept doing that.

Patrick used to do the exact same thing with real estate using sandwich lease options. Same principle. Different asset class.

Here's the key: You keep ratcheting up. You keep buying bigger and bigger things. Eventually, you start buying appreciating assets—things that grow in value over time.

Eventually, you have enough money to buy a piece of real estate.

Eventually, you have enough for oil and gas stocks.

Eventually, you have enough to buy a cash-flowing business.

You just keep scaling up.

But you have to start somewhere. And starting with $250 in your pocket to hit yard sales on Saturday mornings is a completely legitimate way to begin.

And guess what...you will see the same principle applies in real estate and business.

4 WAYS TO GET TO $300K

These are ideas that can be done in the evenings and weekends to escape the rat race. We, Patrick and Robert, have done all of the following and have made at least $1M in each of them across our journey. In other words, they are all valid ways to reach $300K in a few years, even if you're starting from scratch.

1. Acquire and/or keep perfecting a specific skill that you can sell as a service. It can be copywriting, video editing, website design, bookkeeping, or any other valuable skill.

2. If you're tech savvy, you can build out AI-first software tools that solve niche problems, and then earn monthly recurring revenue (MRR) from the people you sell the software to.

3. Start eCommerce Stores. We recommend high ticket items only because the hassle and time spent selling small items in most cases is simply not worth it.

4. Create and/or market digital products. You can create your own courses, books, or tools if you have expertise in certain areas, or you can resell someone else's. This can also lead to consulting opportunities, with much higher margins. The big three are helping people in health, wealth and relationships. Robert and Patrick have both made millions from this method.

3 CORE PRINCIPLES FOR BUILDING ASSETS

Here are three principles that have made us and our clients millions:

1. BUY APPRECIATING ASSETS

Not all assets are equal. Some go up in value over time. Some go down. Some stay flat.

Appreciating assets include:

- Real estate in growing markets
- Stocks in strong companies
- Businesses with growth potential
- Land in good areas
- Certain collectibles (though we don't recommend this for most people)

Depreciating assets include the vast majority of:

- Cars
- Electronics
- Most consumer goods

If you're trying to build wealth, you need to accumulate appreciating assets. Every dollar you spend should go there.

2. SUPPLY & DEMAND MISMATCHES

This is where real money is made. Find opportunities where:

- The seller needs to sell quickly (lower price)
- You know there's a buyer market willing to pay more (high demand, higher price)
- You can position yourself in the middle

That yard sale strategy? That's a supply/demand mismatch.

The real estate deal Robert mentioned? Same thing. His friend needed cash fast (low price). The open market had buyers willing to pay $1.1 million (high demand).

Look for these mismatches everywhere. In your industry. In your local market. In online marketplaces. They exist constantly.

3. BORROW AGAINST APPRECIATING ASSETS

This is what the wealthy do. We don't sell things.

Once you own a piece of real estate or an appreciating stock portfolio, try everything you can to never sell it. Never. Unless there's a very, very strategic reason.

Why? Because selling triggers taxes. And you lose the ongoing appreciation.

Instead, take tax-free loans against your appreciating assets.

If you need money, you can get a line of credit against your real estate equity. You can borrow against your stock portfolio. You can use your 401k as collateral.

The wealthy do this constantly. They buy an asset. It appreciates. They borrow against it tax-free. They use that money to buy more appreciating assets. Repeat.

And if you *must* sell an asset, make sure you're aware of tax strategies:

- **1031 Exchange** - Allows you to defer capital gains taxes by rolling the proceeds into another similar asset (primarily for real estate)
- **Deferred Sales Trust** - A way to defer capital gains taxes when selling any kind of asset by placing proceeds into a trust and reinvesting

As a note here, we're not going to go into the exact strategies of how to legally defer taxes to keep, re-invest, and enjoy more of your capital gains because as our country evolves, so do the legal boundaries in which we operate.

As such, any strategies we outline now, that are adding millions to our clients' bottom lines, might not work two years from now. By then we'll have updated strategies.

For our most up-to-date tax efficiency strategies, just follow the link in the Resources section of this book.

These vehicles can save you hundreds of thousands in taxes. Use them.

TAX-ADVANTAGED SAVINGS VEHICLES

Here are practical accounts and vehicles you should be using to accumulate your $300,000.

401(K) PLANS

If your employer offers a 401(k) with a match, this is the first place your money should go. Period.

The employer match is free money. If they match 6%, you contribute 6%. That's an immediate 100% return on your money.

However—and this is important—maximize the match, but don't put any more into it after that.

There have been tons of studies showing that you're often better off taking additional investment dollars and putting them into different investment vehicles where you have more control and better growth potential.

401(k)s are amazing for the match. Beyond that, there are better options.

ROTH IRA

For most people, a Roth IRA is the way to go for retirement savings beyond the 401(k) match.

The difference between a Roth IRA and a traditional IRA:

- **Traditional IRA**: You get a tax deduction now, but pay taxes when you withdraw in retirement
- **Roth IRA**: You pay taxes now, but all growth and withdrawals in retirement are tax-free

Most people should choose the Roth. You pay the taxes now when you're in a lower tax bracket, and you never pay taxes on the growth. That's powerful over 20-30 years.

Again, any recommendations we make at the writing of this book might not be the absolute best 2 years from now. For our most up-to-date recommendations on savings vehicles, just follow the link in the Resources section of this book.

TAXABLE INVESTMENT ACCOUNTS (STOCKS)

Beyond tax-advantaged accounts, you should be building a taxable investment account with stocks, ETFs, or index funds.

Here's something critical to understand: You only pay taxes on gains when you sell the stock.

If you buy $10,000 of S&P 500 index funds and it grows to $50,000 over 20 years, you don't owe any taxes until you sell.

And remember principle #3: The wealthy don't sell. They borrow against their stock portfolio when they need cash.

You can get a line of credit using your stocks as collateral. The interest rate might be 8-10% annually. But if your stocks are growing at 12-15% annually, you're still making money.

More importantly, you're not triggering capital gains taxes. And your stocks keep growing.

CERTIFICATES OF DEPOSIT (CDs)

CDs are ultra-safe, but they typically offer lower returns. They're essentially loans you make to a bank in exchange for a fixed interest rate over a set period (3 months, 1 year, 5 years, etc.).

Here's a simple strategy for deciding between CDs and stocks:

Check what the S&P 500 forecast is for the next year. Check what the CD rate is.

If the S&P forecast is at least twice the CD rate, put your money in the S&P 500. The S&P rarely underperforms forecasts by more than 50%, so you'll likely beat the CD.

If the S&P forecast is uncertain or volatile, and you want guaranteed returns, go with the CD.

REAL ESTATE

We've already mentioned real estate several times, but it deserves emphasis.

Real estate is one of the best wealth-building vehicles available because:

- It appreciates over time
- You can use it as leverage (mortgages)
- It can generate cash flow (rental income)
- You get tax advantages (depreciation)
- You can borrow against equity tax-free

If you can afford to buy rental property, do it. Start with one. Then another. Keep scaling.

Even if you can't afford property in expensive markets, look at other options. In Romania, for example, you can buy agricultural land and rent it to farmers. They pay you rent annually just to use your land for crops. Same principle, different market.

WHY THIS MATTERS

Every principle we've taught you in this book—from creating your balance sheet to taking 100% responsibility—has been building toward this moment.

You need $300,000 in liquid or semi-liquid assets to access the next level of wealth building.

Part Two of this book will show you how to turn that $300,000 into $3 million, $10 million, or more through strategic business acquisitions.

You can't do any of that without the cash to get started.

If you implement even half of what we've taught you in these first ten chapters, you'll get there faster than you think.

For most people, it takes 5-10 years to accumulate $300,000 in assets if they're starting from zero. Every principle in Part One can cut months or even years off that timeline.

Here's something that might surprise you: In theory, a 12-year-old could pick up this book, implement everything in Part One, and become a millionaire before they turn 20.

We're not exaggerating.

If a young person starts applying these principles at age 12—creating their personal balance sheet, choosing their path, learning to understand others, modeling masters, implementing How Sessions, prioritizing ruthlessly, managing their life energy, networking strategically, taking 100% responsibility, and building toward $300K in assets—they could achieve millionaire status by 18 or 19.

More so, at that point, they could become a client of Elkridge Advisors and leverage our acquisition strategies to become a deca-millionaire (someone worth $10 million or more) by age 25.

Does that sound impossible? It's not.

The math works. The principles work. Time is the most powerful wealth-building tool that exists. Every year you delay implementing these principles costs you exponentially in compound growth.

That's why this chapter—and this entire Part One—exists. To give you the roadmap to get to $300K in assets, regardless of where you're starting from.

Once you get there, Part Two will show you how to turn that $300K into millions through business acquisition.

ACTION STEPS

1. **Prepare your personalized wealth allocation strategy.** Everyone reading this book has a different starting point, different income level, different expenses, different career situations. That means the strategies in this chapter will apply differently to each of you. Your job is to identify which specific tactics from this chapter make sense for YOU right now, and build them into your wealth allocation strategy. Here's how:

- **If you're starting with less than $10K in assets**: Focus on the arbitrage strategies. Go to yard sales this weekend. Find items you can flip for profit. Start with $100-$500 and ratchet up from there. Maximize any employer 401(k) match (free money). Open a Roth IRA and contribute whatever you can, even if it's just $50/month.

- **If you have $10K-$50K in assets**: Continue the arbitrage approach but scale up. Look for bigger opportunities—real estate sandwich leases, wholesale deals, tax sale properties. Aggressively reduce high-interest debt. Max out your 401(k) match. Increase Roth IRA contributions. Start building your real estate or business investment knowledge.

- **If you have $50K-$150K in assets**: You're in the acceleration phase. Consider your first small real estate investment (house hacking, rental property, or partnership). Explore stock leverage strategies (borrowing against securities to invest in appreciating assets). Implement tax-advantaged strategies like 1031 exchanges if selling real estate. Network with people who are already at $300K+ and learn their strategies.

- **If you have $150K-$300K in assets**: You're close. Double down on what's working. If real estate has been your path, acquire another property. If business income has been your path, invest in scaling or acquiring a small business. Prepare for the transition to Part Two. You're 6-18 months away from getting on the Fast Track.

Whatever your starting point, write down your personalized wealth allocation strategy this week. Be specific:

"I will do X, Y, and Z from this chapter because they align with my current situation. My goal is to reach $300K in assets by [specific date]."

1. **Update your balance sheet with your $300K goal and timeline.** Based on your current assets (from Chapter 1) and your monthly savings rate, calculate how long it will take you to reach $300,000. Review it weekly.

2. **Take one arbitrage action this month.** Don't just read about Gary Vaynerchuk's ratcheting-up strategy—do it. Find one item at a yard sale, thrift store, or if you have more cash, an estate sale where you can buy low and sell high. Negotiate well and execute the deal. Learn the fundamentals of value arbitrage through action, not theory.

3. **Maximize your 401(k) match, but don't contribute beyond the match.** If your employer offers a match, take it—that's free money with an instant 50-100% return. But don't put any additional money beyond the match into your 401(k).

4. **Open and fund a Roth IRA if you don't have one.** Even if you can only contribute $100/month, start now. Time in the market beats timing the market.

5. **Learn about tax-advantaged wealth strategies.** Research 1031 exchanges, Deferred Sales Trusts, and lending against appreciating assets. Even if you're not ready to use these strategies yet, understanding how they work now will pay massive dividends later. Knowledge now prevents costly mistakes later, when you have more capital.

6. **Implement one cash-flowing asset strategy.** Whether it's rental real estate, dividend-paying stocks, a side business, or agricultural land rental, acquire ONE cash-flowing asset in the next 90 days. Start small if necessary, but start. The experience you gain is worth

more than the initial return.

7. **Review this chapter monthly until you hit $300K.** Come back to Part One every 30 days. Ask yourself: "What else from these chapters can I implement now? What did I miss the first time?" Different strategies will become relevant at different stages of your journey.

Remember: In theory, a 12-year-old could follow this roadmap and become a millionaire by 20. If you're older than 12, you have more resources, more experience, and more earning power than a child. The only question is: Will you actually do the work?

Your first $300,000 is the hardest money you'll ever make. After that, money makes money. Assets generate returns. Opportunities multiply.

But you have to get to that first milestone.

Everything you've learned so far gives you the roadmap. Now it's time to execute.

Part Two awaits. Let's get you there.

PART II

TURN ASSETS INTO PASSIVE INCOME

"If you don't find a way to make money while you sleep, you will work until you die."
– Warren Buffett.

Welcome to Part Two.

If you've completed Part One and reached $300,000 in assets, congratulations. You're now in a position that most people never reach. You have capital. You have options. You have the ability to make your money work for you instead of just working for money.

Part Two is where the real acceleration happens.

In Part One, you built your foundation. In Part Two, you'll deploy that capital strategically to double your net worth and passive income year after year.

Part Two is split into two main sections:

ACQUIRE

How to find, evaluate, and buy cash-flowing businesses.

In this section, we'll primarily focus on the buyer's interest. However, as you'll notice, we - Patrick and Robert - believe both sides should get maximum value from a transaction. So we've added many tips for those of you who own businesses and are thinking of possibly selling at some point.

All notes for buyers will help you make the safest and most ROI-focused decisions.

Notes for sellers will help you get the best possible price for your asset(s), whilst also reducing acquisition risk for buyers.

Everyone wins. And that's the point of a well-conducted M&A transaction.

Or at least that's what we at Elkridge Advisors believe.

AUTOMATE

How to systematize and scale those businesses to run without you.

Both buyers and sellers will find immense value in ensuring their business assets operate at the highest levels of excellence possible.

That is what we will outline, step by step, in this chapter.

Together, these two strategies create a wealth-building machine that compounds faster than almost any other investment vehicle available.

This next section is primarily Patrick's domain. He's completed over $200 million in business transactions, helped clients build multi-million dollar portfolios, and developed the acquisition strategies we're about to share with you.

One critical note before we begin: In the United States, you can turn every dollar into passive income. The opportunities we're about to show you are accessible to anyone with capital and the willingness to learn the process.

Ready? Let's begin

CHAPTER 11

ACQUIRE

Before you buy a single business, you need to answer one question:

What's your exit strategy?

Most people approach business acquisition backwards. They see an opportunity, get excited, buy it, and then figure out what to do with it later.

That's exactly how you build a portfolio of jobs instead of a wealth-generating empire.

The right way? Start with the end in mind.

Before you ever look at your first deal, before you call your first business owner, before you write your first Letter of Intent, you need to know:

- Are you building for cash flow or for a windfall exit?
- Are you buying one business to replace your W-2 income?
- Or are you building a consolidation strategy to sell to private equity for $50 million+?

These are fundamentally different strategies. They require different types of businesses, different financing structures, and different operational approaches.

THE $10 TRILLION OPPORTUNITY

Before we show you the numbers, you need to understand why this moment in history is unlike any other for acquiring businesses.

We're in the middle of the largest transfer of wealth in American history.

Over the next decade, more than $10 trillion worth of businesses will change hands in the United States. Over half of those businesses are owned by Americans over 50 years of age—primarily baby boomers.

And here's the critical part: **their children and grandchildren don't want these businesses.**

Think about that for a second. A generation ago, if you owned a successful plumbing company, HVAC business, or manufacturing operation, you'd hand it down to your kids. They'd take over. Keep it in the family. That was the American way.

Not anymore.

Today's younger generation has watched their parents and grandparents grind for decades. They've seen the stress. The long hours. The constant pressure. They've seen what business ownership costs.

And they've decided they don't want it.

They want lifestyle. They want to travel. They want work-life balance. They want a 9-to-5 job with weekends off and four weeks of vacation. They want to stare at their phones without worrying about payroll or customer complaints or equipment breaking down at 2am.

This creates a massive opportunity—and a massive problem.

THE BROKEN BROKER SYSTEM

Here's something most people don't know: Less than 20% of businesses listed with brokers actually sell.

This bears repeating: **Under 20% of businesses put on the market with brokers ever close.**

Why is this number so low?

Because the system is fundamentally broken. Brokers get paid 10% commission on the sale price for most small businesses. So they're incentivized to list businesses as high as possible—whether that price is realistic or not.

You'll see businesses listed for 5-6X EBITDA when comparable companies are selling for 3X. They list it high, market it to dozens of buyers, and hope someone bites.

Most of these overpriced businesses sit on the market for 6-12 months before the price gets knocked down to reality.

THE AMATEUR BUYER PROBLEM

Here's where it gets worse.

Over the last few years, educators like Codie Sanchez and Carl Allen have been teaching courses on buying small businesses. They're putting solid information out there—which is great—but they're creating a wave of amateur buyers who get just enough knowledge to be dangerous.

These folks get excited. They learn the basics. Then they go out and start throwing full-price offers at overpriced deals.

Here's what happens:

1. Amateur buyer sees a business listed at $2 million (overpriced at 6X EBITDA)

2. Gets excited and submits a full-price Letter of Intent

3. Seller accepts (of course they do—it's overpriced! "Wow, the Broker was right, I got the price they said I would! Look at me, it worked, I am going to be rich!")

4. Buyer gets an "accepted LOI" and celebrates

5. Moves into due diligence and submits for bank financing

6. The bank runs the numbers and says: "This doesn't work. We'll lend you money, but you need to come up with another $270,000 cash down because the business won't support the debt."

7. Amateur buyer doesn't have an additional $270,000 on hand.

8. Deal falls apart

9. Business goes back on the market at a reduced price

We see this happen all the time.

The result? The market is cluttered with inexperienced buyers bidding up prices, creating false expectations for sellers, and wasting everyone's time.

Meanwhile, certain industries—particularly HVAC, plumbing, and electrical contracting—have become oversaturated with these "looky-loo" buyers. Everyone thinks "boring businesses" means plumbing or HVAC because that's what they heard in a course.

So supply and demand drives up prices in those specific sectors, even though the fundamentals haven't changed.

This is actually good news for you.

Why? Because if you know what you're doing—if you understand deal structure, financing, due diligence, and valuation—you can avoid these overpriced, picked-over deals entirely.

OFF-MARKET DEALS

There's a huge surplus of businesses with no obvious succession plan. And baby boomer owners are looking for exit strategies, but they're not all listing with brokers.

In fact, most quality businesses never hit the public market.

Private equity firms are circling—but they won't touch most of these deals. Why? Because most of these businesses are too small. Private equity typically wants businesses doing at least $3 million and above in EBITDA. Anything below that threshold is "too much hassle, too disorganized, too much stress."

That leaves a massive gap in the market—and that's where you come in.

These businesses are available at discounts if you know where to look. Some are being liquidated at auctions. Others are listed by brokers and have been sitting for six months with reduced prices. Many more are off-market deals where owners would sell to the right buyer who will take care of their legacy and their employees.

At Elkridge Advisors we focus almost exclusively on off-market deals. We reach out directly to business owners. We build relationships. We structure creative deals without broker commissions eating into everyone's profit.

We do target on-market deals, but they typically have to be "seasoned deals" where the business has been on the market for 6 or more months and have likely dropped in price a few times.

Other off market deals we get from dozens, if not hundreds of sources, starting from our network of intermediaries and professionals like CPA's and business attorneys, to our extensive outreach efforts over email, phone calls, texts, social media, physical letters, and everything in between.

When a deal does not have a broker, you can often net the seller the same amount while paying less for the business. A $2 million sale with a 10% broker fee means the seller nets $1.8 million. Offer them $1.85 million direct, and everyone wins. This is just one negotiation strategy in a hat of many we will discuss later, and a great reason to go direct to the Seller.

THE MODERNIZATION OPPORTUNTY

Here's what makes this even better: Most boomer businesses are antiquated.

They're run by 60-70+ year old owners who don't want to upset the apple cart. They're thinking about retirement, not disruption. They're not implementing AI. They're not embracing automation. They don't have sophisticated technology or systems.

Many don't even have formal marketing or sales systems—they've grown entirely through referrals over 20-30 years.

This creates two powerful opportunities:

1. **You can acquire these businesses at low multiples** (3-4X EBITDA or less) because they're small, under-systematized, and have limited buyer interest.

2. **You can dramatically increase their value** by installing modern systems, automation, marketing, and sales processes—often doubling or tripling profits within 2-3 years.

Then, when you consolidate multiple businesses under one entity and sell to private equity at a 6-7X multiple (or more), you've doubled or tripled your money through what we call Acquisitions Arbitrage™.

Graphic: Acquisitions Arbitrage™.

The math is simple but powerful: Buy businesses at 3X, systematize them, consolidate them, grow them, and sell at 7X.

For every $1 million in EBITDA you acquire through additional acquisitions, the enterprise value becomes $2 million when consolidated.

This opportunity won't last forever.

In 5-10 years, the baby boomer wave will have passed. These businesses will have been sold, shut down, or absorbed by larger companies. The arbitrage opportunity will narrow. The amateur buyers will either become professionals or drop out.

But right now? Right now is the golden age of business acquisition for individual investors and entrepreneurs who understand this playbook and can navigate around the noise.

YOUR $60 MILLION ROADMAP

Before we dive into the mechanics of finding and buying businesses, we need to show you something that changes everything for our clients at Elkridge Advisors.

Every week, Robert and Patrick sit down to do strategy sessions with potential clients. These are successful people—executives with 25 years in corporate America, entrepreneurs with $300K-$1M in assets, real estate investors looking to diversify.

They're smart. They're driven. They understand business and investing.

But when we walk them through the Elkridge Financial Model, showing them the exact numbers of what acquiring businesses can do for their net worth over 10 years, their jaws drop.

"Oh my gosh," they say. Every single time.

Here's why:

THE THREE SCENARIOS

Here's the framework we use in strategy sessions. We plug in people's actual net worth estimates and show them three different 10-year scenarios:

SCENARIO 1: CURRENT RETIREMENT PATH

This is where they end up if they keep doing exactly what they're doing now—saving in their 401k, maybe investing in some stocks or real estate, climbing the corporate ladder or running their existing business.

SCENARIO 2: ONE ACQUISITION

This is what happens if they buy just one cash-flowing business using SBA financing and let it run for 10 years while paying down debt. Then we estimate what their net worth will be if we grow and scale the business together. That alone is life changing.

SCENARIO 3: TEN ACQUISITIONS

This is the full Elkridge strategy—acquiring one business per year for 10 years, implementing a roll-up strategy, and building an enterprise worth tens of millions.

Here's a real example.

FROM $2.5M TO $70M IN 10 YEARS

Meet "John" (name changed for confidentiality). Here's his actual situation when he came to us:

Your current financial situation:

- Annual Income (after tax): $300,000
- Cash savings: $250,000
- Stocks/Crypto: $150,000
- Business Equity: $0
- Real Estate Equity: $1,400,000
- 401k/IRA: $750,000
- Current Net Worth: $2,550,000
- Desired Net Worth at Retirement (10 years): $20,000,000
- Current Delta: -$17,450,000

John is 45 years old. He makes good money. He's been responsible with his finances. And yet... at his current trajectory, he's nowhere close to his retirement goal.

Now let's run the three scenarios.

For the sake of simplicity, we will assume:

1. All asset types grow at a 7% per year,
2. Expenses are at $210,000/year (This includes taxes and everything

from cars, vacations, children's education, etc.),

3. 30% of cash generated during the 10 years is reinvested strategically across stocks, real estate, and 401k/IRA.

SCENARIO 1: CURRENT PATH

If John changes nothing and continues his current strategy for 10 years:

- Annual Income: $300,000/year
- Cash grows to: $250,000
- Stocks/Crypto grows to: $709,566 (incl. monthly contributions)
- Business Equity: $0
- Real Estate Equity: $3,168,505 (incl. additional purchases)
- 401k/IRA: $1,889,857 (incl. monthly contributions)

Net Worth in 10 Years: $6,017,928.

He doubles his net worth. Not bad, right? Most people would be happy with that.

Except he's still $13,982,072 short of his $20 million goal...

SCENARIO 2: ONE ACQUISITION

Now let's say John uses his savings and borrowing power to acquire just one business.

Acquisition Details:

- Purchase Price: $4,810,000
- Annual Revenue: $6,500,000
- EBITDA Multiple: 3.7X
- Profit Margin: 20%
- Seller's Discretionary Earnings: $1,300,000

Financing Structure:

- Seller Financing (10%): $481,000
- Seller Standby Note (5%): $240,500
- Buyer Equity Required (5%): $240,500
- SBA Loan (80%): $3,848,000

John's actual cash required: $240,500.

The business generates $613,006 in annual cash flow after all debt service. After you pay a Management Team $200,000 to run the business for you, you are at $413k cash flow per year. Not bad for a $240k investment... A 172% ROI in year 1.

Over 10 years:

- Annual passive income: $709,611 (after paying General Manager + debt service)
- Business equity grows to: $4,344,000 (debt paid down, business appreciated)
- Other assets also grow quicker as a result of additional contributions from discretionary passive income

Net Worth in 10 Years: $15,446,095.

Now John is only $4,553,905 short of his goal, with just one $240K investment. Much better.

By the way, John does not grow the business he acquired at all. If he would have grown it even just a bit every year, it's VERY likely that in 10 years he would have more than doubled revenue and profit. In that case, John would have passed his $20 million goal.

But watch what happens with the full strategy:

SCENARIO 3: TEN ACQUISITIONS

Same financing structure, but John acquires one business per year for 10 years following the consolidation thesis.

The magic of multiple arbitrage kicks in:

- He buys small businesses at 2-4X EBITDA
- He consolidates them into a platform
- The combined enterprise sells at 6-7X EBITDA or higher

After 10 years:

- Annual passive income: $3,977,190
- Cash position: $13,465,632
- Business equity value: $45,840,000
- Other assets: $2,249,197 (401k) + $5,572,862 (real estate) + $3,113,922 (stocks)

Net Worth in 10 Years: $70,241,613.

John exceeds his goal by $50,241,613.

From $2.5M to $70M in 10 years.

That's the "On my gosh!" moment. Once again, this assumes you have not scaled the business at all after acquisition. When you factor realistic growth, the exit can easily be north of $120M.

Net Worth Paths	No Acquisition	One Acquisition	Ten Acquisitions
Annual Income			
Active	$300,000	$300,000	$300,000
Passive	$0	$709,611	$3,977,190
Net Worth			
Cash On Hand	$250,000	$3,697,527	$13,465,632
401k/IRA	$1,889,857	$2,249,197	$2,249,197
Stocks	$709,566	$1,348,216	$3,113,922
Real Estate Equity	$3,168,505	$3,807,155	$5,572,862
Business Equity	$0	$4,344,000	$45,840,000
Total Net Worth	**$6,017,928**	**$15,446,095**	**$70,241,613**
Delta To $20M Goal	- $13,982,072	- $4,553,905	+ $50,241,613

Graphic: Net Worth Growth Paths.

WHY THIS MODEL WORKS

This isn't fantasy. This isn't MLM. This isn't get-rich-quick.

Here's why the math works:

1. LEVERAGE

You're using 95% borrowed money (SBA loans + seller financing). Your $180K down payment controls a $3.6M asset.

2. THE BUSINESS PAYS FOR EVERYTHING

The business cash flow covers all debt service. You're not paying anything out of pocket except the initial down payment.

3. MULTIPLE ARBITRAGE

As you consolidate businesses, the combined enterprise becomes worth more per dollar of EBITDA. Buy at 3-4X, sell at 6-7X.

4. DEBT PAYDOWN

Every year, the business pays down the loan. In 10 years, you own it free and clear (or you've sold it for a massive exit).

5. COMPOUNDING

Each acquisition builds on the previous ones. By year 5, you have significant cash flow to use for additional acquisitions and growth.

THE REALISTIC EXPECTATIONS TALK

Now, we must be completely honest with you.

The model we just showed you is mathematically accurate. It's based on real deal structures we use every day. We've had clients achieve results very close to this.

But....

...it will not be a smooth ride.

You will hit roadblocks. Deals will fall through. Businesses will have problems. Employees will quit. Customers will leave. Equipment will break. The economy will have ups and downs.

The world will try to stop you from achieving this.

That's why persistence and consistency are everything. That's why having the right systems (Robert's expertise) and the right acquisition strategy (Patrick's expertise) matters so much.

We're not promising this will be easy. We're promising it's worth it, and it's possible—if you do the work.

THE REAL ESTATE COMPARISON

Here's some context that makes this opportunity even clearer.

We ask investors thinking about working with us a simple question:

Knowing what you know now... if you could go back 20 years and beg, borrow and plead for as much money as possible to buy every piece of real estate you could possibly buy... would you?

Of course you would.

If you bought a house in 2004 for $500,000, what would it be worth today?

In most markets probably $1.5 million. Maybe $2 million if you're in a hot market.

It would have tripled.

If you bought five of those properties, you'd have a $7.5 million portfolio.

You can do the same thing right now with business acquisitions, but with significantly larger returns.

Why?

Real estate loans are 30-year mortgages. If you bought property 20 years ago, you still have 10 years of payments left until it's free and clear

Business loans are 10-year loans. And the business pays for everything except your down payment.

Let's break this down with real numbers:

Say you buy two businesses this year and next year. Each costs $5 million. Each generates $1 million in EBITDA.

Over 10 years:

- The business itself pays off the $5 million loan (not you)
- You collect the $1 million per year in EBITDA (minus loan payments, but still substantial cash flow)
- After 10 years, you own both businesses free and clear
- You sell them for $15-20 million total (based on growth and

multiples)

Your total cash flow over 10 years plus sale proceeds can easily exceed $10-15 million, with minimal capital invested upfront.

Compare that to real estate where you're still making payments 20 years later and hoping for appreciation.

Simply put: Business acquisitions compound wealth much faster.

MULTIPLE ARBITRAGE: THE FOUNDATION

Before we go any further, you need to understand the single most important concept in business acquisitions: multiple arbitrage.

This is the engine that makes everything work.

Here's the principle:

Small businesses (under $5M revenue) typically sell for 3-4X EBITDA.

Larger businesses ($10M+ revenue) sell for 5-7X EBITDA or higher.

But what happens when you consolidate?

Example:

You buy five businesses over five years:

- Each generates $1M in EBITDA
- You pay 3.5X EBITDA for each = $3.5M per business
- Total investment: $17.5M (mostly financed)
- Combined EBITDA: $5M

Now you have a consolidated platform generating $5M in EBITDA. This is no longer a "small business." This is a mid-market company.

What's it worth?

At 6X EBITDA (conservative for a mid-market company): $30 million

You bought $17.5M worth of businesses and created $30M in enterprise value. That's $12.5M in value creation through consolidation alone—before any operational improvements, synergies, or growth.

That's multiple arbitrage.

And it's 100% legal, ethical, and how private equity firms make billions of dollars every year.

The difference? They do it with institutional capital. You can do it with SBA loans.

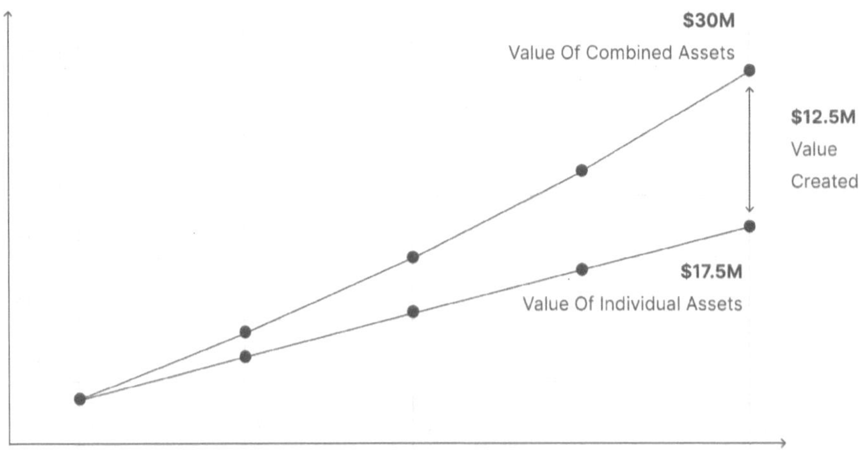

Graphic: Multiple Arbitrage Value Creation.

SBA LOANS: THE GAME-CHANGER

The Small Business Administration (SBA) has created the most powerful wealth-building opportunity in America right now, and most people don't even know it exists.

Here's what you need to know:

STANDARD SBA LOAN TERMS

- 10% down payment (vs. 20-30% for conventional business loans)
- 10-year loan term
- The business cash flow pays for everything after your down payment

That's already powerful. But it gets better.

THE SBA 5% DOWN STRATEGY

The SBA now allows you to buy businesses with as little as 5% cash injection if you structure the deal correctly.

Here's how it works:

The SBA requires 10% total equity injection. But they're willing to let half of that (5%) come from the seller through something called a 10-year standby note.

A standby note means:

- The seller agrees to take 5% of the purchase price as a note
- That note accrues interest for 10 years but has no monthly payments
- At the end of 10 years, you make a balloon payment

Example:

You want to buy a $5 million business.

- Traditional approach: $500K down (10%)
- SBA 5% strategy: $250K down (5% cash) + $250K standby note from seller (5% deferred)

That's half the cash required upfront.

And here's the kicker: Sellers almost always agree to this because they still get their full purchase price, just with a small portion deferred.

This is how you can buy multiple businesses without needing millions in capital.

This is how you can deploy your $300K into a $3-5 million business that generates $500K-$1M per year in cash flow.

This is how you build generational wealth starting with capital most people can achieve in a few years.

Once you own a business, it gets even better.

If you already own a business in a given industry, like a roofing company, or you just acquired one, the SBA has something called the Business Expansion Program (BEP).

Under this program, if you qualify personally, you currently own a healthy business and are acquiring a healthy business in the same industry, you may qualify for the BEP loan, **which is 0% down!**

As long as the total SBA Series 7(a) loan in any specific industry, or SIC code is less than $5 million, you can acquire that business for $0 out of pocket.

The concept here is that it is all about risk to the bank and SBA. If you have already proven yourself as being able to successfully run a similar sized business in the same industry, then the risk to them is much lower, hence the possibility of acquiring a business with no cash down.

SBA VS. CONVENTIONAL FINANCING

Here's a break-down of the differences so you can understand why we prioritize SBA loans:

SBA 7(a) Loans:

- Down payment: 5-10%
- Loan amount: Up to $5 million
- Interest rate: Currently around 9.5-10%
- Term: 10 years
- Seller financing: Encouraged (up to 15-20%)
- Business cash flow: Covers debt service

Conventional Business Loans:

- Down payment: 20-30%
- Loan amount: Varies by lender
- Interest rate: Sometimes lower (7-9%)
- Term: Varies (often 5-7 years)
- Seller financing: Limited

- Personal guarantee: Almost always required

WHY SBA WINS:

The lower down payment means you can acquire more businesses with the same capital. That's the key to building a portfolio quickly.

Yes, conventional loans sometimes have better rates. But the cash efficiency of SBA loans makes them far superior for wealth building.

The shorter term of a conventional business loan also makes the cash flow much less than an SBA loan during the repayment period.

Thus it's much harder to acquire a company and cash flow it with a conventional loan. But, on the upside of that, if you don't need the cash flow, then the business will basically pay for itself much quicker, giving you more equity every month, and reaching a much higher cashflow once the loan is paid off.

KEY REQUIREMENTS FOR SBA APPROVAL

Not every business qualifies for SBA financing. Here's what lenders look for:

The Business:

- Operating for at least 2 years
- Profitable (positive cash flow). They typically like to see above 15% profit margin, but varies by industry.
- Clean financial statements
- No major litigation or liens

- Located and operating in the U.S.

The Buyer:

- Credit score of 680+ (ideally 700+)
- Management experience in the industry or related field OR acquire a business where the current management team remains in place.
- Personal liquidity (typically 5-10% of loan amount in reserves)
- Clean background check
- U.S. citizen or eligible visa status

The Deal Structure:

- Debt Service Coverage Ratio (DSCR) of at least 1.25 (ideally 1.5+)
- Reasonable purchase price relative to cash flow
- Adequate collateral
- Proper use of proceeds

We'll cover DSCR and deal structuring in detail later in this chapter.

CHOOSE YOUR PATH

Now that you understand the financial framework and financing options, let's talk about strategy.

There are two primary approaches to business acquisition, and you should choose which one aligns with your goals.

STRATEGY 1: BUY-AND-HOLD FOR CASH FLOW

Goal: Replace your W-2 income and create passive income streams netting you 7-figures yearly.

Approach:

- Buy one or a few businesses
- Implement systems so they run without you
- Collect cash flow for years or decades
- Maybe sell eventually, maybe pass to heirs

Ideal for:

- People who want financial freedom without a big exit
- Those who enjoy being business owners
- Individuals comfortable with 7-figure net worth goals

Typical businesses:

- Service businesses with recurring revenue
- B2B companies with long-term contracts
- Established lifestyle businesses

Exit timeline: No rush. 10-20+ years, or never.

STRATEGY 2: ROLL-UP FOR WINDFALL EXIT

Goal: Build an empire worth $50M-$200M+ and sell to private equity or a strategic buyer.

Approach:

- Identify a fragmented industry
- Buy a platform company
- Acquire 5-15 complementary businesses (tuck-ins)
- Consolidate operations, eliminate redundancies
- Grow EBITDA aggressively
- Sell the entire portfolio to private equity at a premium multiple

Ideal for:

- Investors who want to build something massive
- Those willing to work intensely for 5-10 years
- People comfortable with complexity and risk
- Individuals with 8-9-figure net worth goals

A Few Typical industries:

- HVAC and plumbing
- Electrical contracting
- Property management

- Home healthcare
- Professional services firms
- Specialty manufacturing

Exit timeline: 5-10 years

THE KEY DIFFERENCE

Buy-and-hold is about cash flow today.

Roll-up is about enterprise value tomorrow.

Both strategies work. Both create wealth. But they require different mindsets, different operational approaches, and different types of businesses.

Before you start looking at businesses, decide which strategy you're pursuing.

Everything else in this chapter depends on that decision.

STEP 1: IDENTIFY YOUR BUY BOX

Your "buy box" is the set of criteria that defines which businesses you'll pursue and which you'll ignore.

Without a clear buy box, you'll waste months chasing deals that don't fit your strategy, don't match your skills, or don't meet your financial requirements.

Here's how to define yours:

CORE BUY BOX CRITERIA

1. Industry/Sector

What type of business do you want to own?

For a buy-and-hold strategy, choose something you understand or have experience in. For a roll-up strategy, choose an industry that's:

- Fragmented (lots of small competitors)
- Recession and AI resistant
- Has recurring revenue potential
- Allows for operational synergies when consolidated

As noted before, some common industries we target are:

- Home services (HVAC, plumbing, electrical) or related supply industries in these verticals. They are just as recession resistant.
- Commercial services (janitorial, landscaping, property management)
- Healthcare services
- Business services
- Specialty manufacturing
- Digital/tech-enabled services

2. Revenue Range

For most first-time buyers: $3M-$7.5M in annual revenue.

Why this range?

- Large enough to support professional management
- Small enough to afford with SBA financing
- Prices typically 3-4X EBITDA

3. EBITDA/Profitability

Minimum: 10% EBITDA margin (15%+ is better)

The business needs to generate enough cash flow to:

- Service debt
- Pay for the General Manager's salary (or for you if you're taking a hands-on management approach)
- Provide return on your investment after the above two

4. Geography

Where can you realistically operate or oversee the business?

For your first acquisition, we recommend:

- Within 2 hours of where you live (especially if you'll be hands-on)
- Anywhere in the U.S. (if you're implementing strong systems and hiring management or buying a business that already has both in place)

For a roll-up strategy, geography matters more. You want:

- Businesses in same or adjacent markets (easier to consolidate)

- Or new platform businesses (see definition in Chapter 13) in complementary locations (national footprint)

5. Customer Base

Look for:

- Diversified customer base (no customer >15% of revenue)
- Recurring revenue or repeat customers
- Long-term contracts (ideal)

Avoid:

- Single customer concentration
- Heavy government contracting (unless that's your expertise)
- Highly seasonal businesses (unless you can manage the cash flow cycles)

6. Growth Potential

Can you grow this business by 20-30% per year?

Look for opportunities to:

- Add sales and marketing systems (many small businesses have zero marketing)
- Expand service offerings
- Enter adjacent markets
- Improve pricing

- Add recurring revenue streams

ADDITIONAL CRITERIA

OWNER DEPENDENCY

Can the business run without the current owner? Or is the owner the business?

For your first acquisition, buy something that already has systems and management in place. Don't buy a job.

TECHNOLOGY/SYSTEMS

Does the business use modern software and systems? Or is everything on paper and in the owner's head?

The more systematized, the better.

COMPETITIVE POSITION

Is this business a leader in its market? Or struggling to survive?

You want businesses with strong reputations, good customer reviews, and competitive advantages.

GROWTH STAGE

Ideal: Mature and stable, but with untapped growth potential.

Avoid: Rapid decline or requires massive capital investment to survive.

WRITE IT DOWN

Take 30 minutes right now and write out your buy box criteria.

Be specific. This document will guide every decision you make for the next 6-12 months.

Example Buy Box:

- Industry: HVAC and plumbing services
- Revenue: $3M-$8M annually
- EBITDA: 12%+ margin
- Geography: Within 100 miles of Dallas, TX
- Customer Base: 70%+ residential recurring service contracts
- Owner Dependency: Owner works 10-20 hours/week in operations
- Growth Potential: No current marketing system in place

That's a clear buy box. Every business you evaluate will either fit or not fit.

You can also use the editable Buy Box Template and App we link to in the Resources section at the end of the book.

STEP 2: SOURCE DEAL FLOW

This is where most aspiring acquirers fail.

They don't know how to find businesses for sale. They rely on brokers, see overpriced deals, get discouraged, and quit.

Let's show you the right way to source deals.

THE BROKER PROBLEM

About 90% of businesses listed with brokers are overpriced, picked over, or have problems.

Why?

Because brokers get paid on commission. They're incentivized to:

- List the price as high as possible
- Market to as many buyers as possible
- Close deals quickly

This creates a bidding war environment where you're competing with dozens of other buyers, all bidding up the price.

It might seem like a good deal for the seller, but in 80% of cases, none of the bidders buy. It just burns all those otherwise great contacts, many of whom might have been more than willing to pay a fair market price, but are now unwilling to pay the broker's made-up price.

We rarely buy from brokers in the first six months a business is listed.

Instead, we focus on off-market deals—businesses that aren't publicly for sale, or deals that are listed with investment bankers. Investment bankers are in another league from brokers, and are more likely to accept a fair price for the business.

OFF-MARKET DEAL SOURCING STRATEGY

Here's how we find businesses before they hit the market:

1. Build a Target List

Once we've defined the buy box—which includes three key elements: industry, size (annual revenue and/or EBITDA), and geography—we can start sourcing deals.

We invest in databases that match these criteria and pull target lists of businesses, including owner emails and/or phone numbers.

2. Direct Outreach Campaigns: The Omnipresent Approach

We use what's called an "omnipresent" marketing and outreach strategy. This means reaching business owners through multiple channels:

- Email outreach
- Direct mail (physical letters)
- Phone calls
- Text messages
- LinkedIn connections

Depending on the deal, we sometimes use up to four different channels to reach owners.

WHY OFF-MARKET DEALS ARE BETTER

Off-market deals have a major advantage: there's no broker involved.

Here's why that matters:

If you're selling a business for $2 million and there's a broker, that's $200,000 in commission out the door. The seller only nets $1.8 million minus their basis.

If we can offer $1.85 million directly, with no broker, the seller nets more than they would at $2 million with a broker—while the acquirer pays less. Everyone wins. The seller avoids the hassle of working through a broker, most of whom don't actually help the business operate better. Most brokers just "package" a business to make it look better.

At Elkridge, when we work with a seller, our Business Operators go in and actually help improve the business. Both the seller and the buyer are much happier with the transaction.

The seller knows their company is in great shape, because they invested in it (and get their money back because they sold it at a better, fairer price).

The buyer knows they're buying a healthier asset.

It's like taking your car to an excellent mechanic right before selling it. You have to invest some money, but you get a much better deal for your car, and your buyer gets a better vehicle.

WHEN TO USE BROKERS

We don't want to give the impression that we never work with brokers. We do. But only for strategic reasons.

Here's when working with a broker makes sense:

1. After six months. If a business has been on the market for six months, the price typically comes down to more realistic levels, and competition has dropped off.

2. For deal flow supplementation. While we focus on off-market deals, we also monitor broker listings for opportunities that might fit our clients' buy boxes. If it's a good deal, it's a good deal, no matter the source.

3. For relationship building. We build relationships with quality brokers and investment bankers who bring us deals before they're publicly listed.

As a principle, the key is not relying on brokers and intermediaries as your primary source. Brokers are great as a supplementary channel, while we focus our energy on off-market outreach.

THE REAL SECRET: PERSISTENCE

Here's the truth about deal sourcing: Most people quit too early.

They send 100 or maybe even 1,000 emails, get a few responses, no immediate deals, and give up.

The people who succeed? They're the ones who send 1,000s of emails. Who makes 1,000 calls. Who mail 300 physical letters. Who keep showing up, month after month.

Buying businesses is not a get-rich-quick scheme. It's a systematic, persistent process that requires discipline and consistency.

But if we stay the course, if we keep reaching out and building relationships, we will find deals.

And when we do, they'll be worth the effort because over the course of a few years, they will add millions to our clients' net worth.

STEP 3: QUALIFY THE OPPORTUNITY

Once we've made contact with a business owner and they're interested in talking, now what?

We qualify the opportunity quickly, whereas amateur buyers waste months on deals that were never going to close.

THE INITIAL CONVERSATION

Your first call with the owner has one goal: Determine if the asset is worth pursuing.

Here are some of the questions we ask:

About the Asset:

- How long have you owned the business?
- What's the current annual revenue?
- What's the profit margin?
- How many employees?
- What's your role in day-to-day operations?

About the Owner's Motivations:

- Why are you considering selling?
- What's your timeline for transition?
- What are you hoping to accomplish with a sale?
- Have you spoken with other buyers or brokers?
- What's your ideal outcome?

Red Flags to Listen For:

- "I'm not really sure I want to sell" = Not motivated
- "I need to get out immediately" = Probably a problem you don't know about yet
- "The business can't run without me" = You're buying a job, not a business
- "We've had some challenges lately" = Declining business

Green Lights to Listen For:

- "I'm ready to retire" = Motivated seller
- "The business runs well with my team" = Systems in place
- "We've been profitable for 10+ years" = Stable business
- "I'm open on price if we can structure it right" = Flexible seller

THE QUALIFICATION CHECKLIST

After the initial conversation, we run through this checklist:

[ ] Revenue fits my buy box

[ ] Owner is truly motivated to sell

[ ] Business has been profitable for 3+ years

[ ] Owner is willing to share financial statements

[ ] Business is not heavily owner-dependent

[ ] Timeline aligns with our goals

[ ] No major red flags emerge

If they check all these boxes, we move forward.

If not, we politely move on. We don't waste time on deals that don't fit.

QUICK BUT IMPORTANT NOTES

Firstly, we want to find out what is most important to the seller. A natural tendency is to assume they care most about the final price. While getting a fair price is important, more often than not price is not the end all be all factor that guides their decision process. In fact, we would argue that the majority of Baby Boomers are concerned more about their legacy, and that their employees are cared for post-acquisition.

It's to your benefit to uncover these points in your conversations with the owner(s). When you gain their trust because you provide what is most important to them, you will likely be able to acquire the business at a better price and/or on better terms. Many times Baby Boomers are independently wealthy and will sacrifice some equity to make sure they have the "right person" taking over their "baby".

Secondly, and for clarity: Owners that are up front and honest about red flags are always preferable to liars who hide them from you.

If the owner says "I can't take this anymore. I've been running this for too long." Yes, that's a red flag. BUT, that same owner might gladly coach a new CEO to replace them.

Also, because of their humble self-analysis, they might be willing to sell the business for a smaller multiple, to make up for some of the negatives.

In other words, for every red flag, there's a solution, and sometimes even an advantage. You just need to understand the risks and efforts involved to make the deal work.

At Elkridge, we take pride in looking at the amazing legacies these entrepreneurs have built, faults and all. And we do them justice by putting in place competent staff and effective systems that take those legacies forward under their new owners.

If you've lived long enough, you know the world isn't all sunshine and rainbows. Even with the absolute best intentions, and all the amount of work we're capable of putting in, things don't always go as planned.

So whenever we look at a company, we seek to understand, rather than criticize.

We analyze data. We calculate probabilities.

If we find that a specific business will need $500,000 to get into shape, but the owner is willing to give our client a $700,000 discount for the inconvenience, that might still be an amazing deal.

This takes time, of course. More than most are willing to put in.

That's why we emphasize across throughout this book: we are not selling get rich quick schemes. Either you, or someone you hire, must do all this work.

Our strategies can make you tens of millions of dollars in just 1-2 decades... if you apply everything correctly.

STEP 4: REVIEW FINANCIAL STATEMENTS

If the opportunity passes initial qualification, it's time to see the numbers.

WHAT TO REQUEST

We ask the owner for:

1. **Last 3 years of Profit & Loss statements**
2. **Last 3 years of tax returns** (business and personal)
3. **Current year-to-date P&L**
4. **Balance Sheet** (most recent)
5. **List of major customers** (revenue by customer)

Most owners will provide P&Ls first, then tax returns after they trust you more.

That's fine. Start with what they're willing to share.

WHAT WE LOOK FOR

Revenue Trends:

- Is revenue growing, stable, or declining?
- Any major fluctuations year to year?
- Seasonality patterns?

Profitability:

- What's the true EBITDA margin?
- Are there one-time expenses that inflate or deflate profit?
- How does the P&L compare to tax returns? (They should match reasonably closely)

Add-Backs:

Many businesses show lower profit on paper than they actually generate because owners run personal expenses through the business.

Common add-backs:

- Owner's salary (if above market rate)
- Personal vehicles
- Personal travel
- Family members on payroll who don't work full-time
- One-time legal or consulting fees

- Owner's health insurance and benefits

Adjusted EBITDA = Reported EBITDA + Legitimate Add-Backs

This is the number that determines the business's true cash-generating ability.

FINANCIAL RED FLAGS

- Declining revenue year over year
- Inconsistent profitability
- Major customer concentration (>15% from one customer)
- Significant difference between P&L and tax returns
- Lack of documentation or disorganized records

FINANCIAL GREEN FLAGS

- Steady or growing revenue
- Consistent 10-15%+ EBITDA margins
- Diversified customer base
- Clean, well-organized financials
- Conservative accounting (better to find hidden value than hidden problems)

STEP 5: CALCULATE VALUATION

Once we have financials, it's time to determine what the business is worth.

There are several valuation methods, but for small to mid-sized businesses, we primarily use two:

METHOD 1: EBITDA MULTIPLE

This is the most common high-level method for businesses under $10M in revenue.

Formula: Enterprise Value = EBITDA × Multiple

The multiple varies greatly based on:

- Industry (SaaS companies get higher multiples than local services)
- Size (larger businesses command higher multiples)
- Growth rate (fast-growing businesses get premium multiples)
- Customer concentration (diversified = higher multiple)
- Owner dependency (less dependent = higher multiple)

Typical Multiples:

- Small local service businesses: 2.5-3.5X EBITDA
- Established service businesses with systems: 3.5-4.5X EBITDA
- Mid-market companies ($5M+ EBITDA): 5-7X EBITDA
- Strategic or high-growth businesses: 6-10X+ EBITDA

Example:

Business generates $1M in adjusted EBITDA. Industry standard multiple: 3.5X Enterprise Value = $1M × 3.5 = $3.5M

At Elkridge Advisors, we only use the above method as an initial rule of thumb, to determine in a few seconds if it even makes sense to do a full DCF Valuation.

In other words, we don't buy or sell companies based on this model of valuation. It's just to get a quick idea of potential value.

Where the EBITDA model falls down is that it doesn't take into consideration the different cash flow levels at the different stages of growth for a particular company. You need to determine whether the company is in a start up phase, sustained growth phase or if it has reached maturity.

Additionally, where people get in trouble is not properly accounting for the differentiation between ACTUAL cash flow and EBITDA alone.

Let's take a quote from the Oracle of Omaha himself, Warren Buffett: "Trumpeting EBITDA is a particularly pernicious practice...people who use EBITDA are either trying to con you or they're conning themselves."

Basing the valuation on EBITDA alone does not properly account for many critical pieces of the equation that determine cash flow. One must account for expenses that will impact cash flow and cash flow cycles. Particularly depreciation, amortization, expected capital expenditures, and working capital (non-cash working capital and cash working capital).

Without accounting for these, everything may look good from a multiple standpoint, but you may find yourself having to pump an additional couple hundred thousands dollars into the business to keep it afloat.

METHOD 2: DISCOUNTED CASH FLOW (DCF)

This method projects future cash flows and discounts them back to present value.

It's more complex but gives you a more accurate picture, especially for businesses with growth potential.

We use the DCF method for all our deals. It is one of the most widely used ways to estimate the intrinsic value of a business.

As a side note: This method is not recommended for beginners. It's highly advised that you have a professional who is a Nationally Certified Business Valuation Expert utilize this method.

Having said that, it is by far the safest method when determining the value of any business, and is why we say "No" to well over 95% of the businesses we look at, while just doing the multiple method might have said "Yes."

As they say: Cash is King.

The DCF valuation method is based on the premise that a company is worth the total amount of cash it can generate in the future, reflected back to today's dollars.

Instead of looking only at current earnings or book value, DCF focuses on the actual free cash flows that the business is expected to produce over time and discounts them to their present value using a discount rate that reflects the current risk and time value of money.

Here is how it works from a 30,000 foot view:

First you forecast what the free cash flow will be for a specific period of time (we use 10 years). Then you discount each years' free cash flow using the formula:

Discounted FCF = FCF (Year T) / (1+R)^T

R = Discount Rate (weighted average cost of capital).

T = Time Period.

Then we sum all FCF's for the periods and add the Terminal Value (TV):

TV = Final Year Cash Flow x (1+G) / (R-G)

G = Perpetual Growth Rate.

We then add up all of the Free Cash Flows and the Terminal Value to get the DCF enterprise value.

In layman's terms, DCF gives you the amount of cash the business would generate over its life, adjusted for the fact that money received in the future is worth less than it is now.

As stated above, one must also properly account for those items that will impact cash flow, such as capital expenditures and working capital.

We won't provide an example here because when we use the DCF method we're also very careful to determine if the company can actually generate the FCF over at least 10 years, based on where the industry is going and how the company is operating. Every industry is different, every operation is different.

METHOD 3: COMPARABLE SALES

We look at recent sales of similar businesses in the same industry and geography.

This is harder to do because most business sale data is private, but business brokers and M&A advisors have access to this data.

THE OFFER RANGE

After we've calculated valuation using multiple methods, we have a range.

Example:

- EBITDA Multiple Method: $3.2M - $3.8M
- DCF Method: $3.5M
- Comparable Sales: $3.0M - $4.0M

Offer range: **$3.2M - $3.8M**

Now we know what the business is worth, but what we actually offer depends on:

- How motivated the seller is
- How competitive the process is
- How much value can be created post-acquisition
- The buyer's financing capacity
- A number of other operational factors we uncover during the due diligence phase.

Generally, our first offer is at the lower end of the range, which leaves room for negotiation.

A NOTE ON FAIRNESS

We could make offers below the fair valuation of an asset. People do it all the time.

At Elkridge, we simply believe what's fair is fair. If your company is worth $2-3M, we advise our clients to not offer anything under $2M.

As we mentioned before, we want both sides to be happy with the arrangement.

Now, if your company is worth $20M, and our client can only go up to $15M, even with a bank loan... well, we'll have to get creative with the offer. It's still doable, and we've closed on many deals before where there were significant differences between value and financial ability.

So don't get discouraged if that ever happens to you. Whether you're the seller or the buyer, know that in this day and age, where there's a will there's a way.

This is why we put in a lot of effort to value companies properly. Our due diligence process typically takes between 30-45 days, depending on the scale and complexity of a company.

This process has an additional, very critical benefit: It prepares the buyer for ownership of the asset.

If a buyer goes through due diligence too quickly, they miss out on acquiring intimate knowledge of the business, its staff, its clients, its culture, and everything in between.

Proper due diligence gets you to a truly fair valuation and it makes it so as soon as the new owner comes in, they already have a very good pulse on their new asset from day one.

STEP 6: STRUCTURE THE DEAL

This is where the art and science of acquisitions come together.

Deal structure is often more important than price. A seller might accept a lower price if the terms are favorable.

Here's how we structure deals at Elkridge:

THE OPTIMAL STRUCTURE

Target Breakdown:

- SBA Loan: 75-80%
- Seller Financing: 10-20%
- Seller Standby Note: 5%
- Buyer Equity: 5-10%

ANATOMY OF A REAL DEAL

Let's take you inside an actual acquisition we're working on right now, as we - Robert and Patrick - write this book.

This is a live deal. We're putting together the Letter of Intent as we write this. (Obviously, all identifying information has been removed).

THE TARGET BUSINESS

Industry: HVAC and Plumbing. **Annual Revenue:** $12,000,000. **Purchase Price:** $7,300,000

THE VALUATION METHOD

Here's something most people get wrong: they think valuation is just "EBITDA times a multiple." That's not how we really value businesses. It's just a metric to compare different businesses.

When you actually value a business, there's so much more that goes into it, as we discussed in the valuation section above.

DEAL STRUCTURE BREAKDOWN

Here's how we're structuring this $7.3 million acquisition:

Cash Down (Buyer Equity): $364,400 (5%)

Seller Financing: $1,571,200 (21.5%)

Seller Standby Note: $364,400 (5%)

SBA Financing: $5,000,000 (68.5%, SBA loans are capped at $5 million, so on larger deals like this, seller financing becomes essential)

WHY THIS STRUCTURE WORKS

The buyer is bringing $364,400 in cash to close a $7.3 million deal—that's only 5% down.

After all debt payments and the cost of running the business (including the cost of new management), the buyer's annual cash flow is conservatively projected to be $650,000.

That's a $650,000 annual return on a $364,400 investment.

Let that sink in for a bit.

Where else can you invest $365K and get $650k in *annual* passive income?

Now, we need to be clear. This is cash flow. That is after everything is already paid for, so no smoke and mirrors. It's actual cash in hand.

If you were to look at EBITDA, you would see an even stronger number, at $1.7m, and Sellers Discretionary Earnings of $2.3m.

But don't let these fool you. That is not cash in the bank. Many Brokers will try to tell you it is.

Cash flow is king, bottom line.

This is precisely where using just the "EBITDA Multiple" method fails. If you were to strictly utilize the multiple method, this business might be valued at $11.5 million. (V=$2.3 million x multiple of 5). If someone tried to pay $11.5 million for this business, they would fail because the cash flow would not be in place to support it.

In this case, there is over $1.8 million in working capital needed for this type of business. And there is a high level of annual capital expenditures required as well. If you don't account for these in your valuation methodology, you'll be sorely disappointed when you go bankrupt, and you might even have to fund from your savings just to keep the doors open.

KEY METRICS LENDERS EVALUATE

When we submit deals to SBA lenders, they're looking at specific metrics. It's critical to understand these:

1. DEBT SERVICE COVERAGE RATIO (DSCR)

Formula: Net Operating Income ÷ Total Annual Debt Service

The bank's minimum is typically 1.2. We won't look at a deal unless it's at least 1.5. If it's over 2.0, we know we've got a strong deal.

Most of our deals fall in the 1.5 to 2.0 range.

For this HVAC deal: The DSCR is approximately 1.7, which is decent and acceptable.

What This Means: DSCR shows how much cushion you have between the cash the business generates, and what you need to pay back in debt. At 1.7, the business generates 1.7 times more cash than needed to service the debt.

2. WORKING CAPITAL CONSIDERATIONS

One thing most people mess up: they don't account for working capital needs and capital expenditures, as we hinted at before.

You must forecast working capital growth over time and account for depreciation and capital expenditures. If you don't understand these, you'll get to the end of the year thinking you made $500K but you only cleared $250K because you didn't realize what capital expenditures are or how working capital needs fluctuate.

3. SELLER FINANCING TERMS

Seller financing typically ranges from 10% to about 30%.

We try to get it as high as possible because:

- We can control the terms better
- The interest rates are usually more favorable than bank rates
- It immediately reduces the capital gains the seller has to pay
- The seller earns interest, like a bank (we often offer 5%, whereas current rates are around 9.5%)

Important Note on Seller Financing:

The SBA will never be subordinate to seller financing. If the business fails, SBA gets paid back first, then the seller. That's why sellers typically don't go much above 40% seller financing—it becomes too risky for them.

4. SBA LOAN LIMITS

SBA will loan up to $5 million maximum per SIC code (Standard Industrial Code). That's why on this deal, we need substantial seller financing—the SBA portion alone can't cover the entire purchase price.

On some deals, you could technically get SBA to go up to 90% financing if they agreed, but we prefer maximizing seller financing when possible for better interest rate terms.

Step 7: THE LETTER OF INTENT (LOI)

Once we've valued the business and agreed on general terms with the seller, we formalize the offer in a Letter of Intent (LOI).

The LOI is **non-binding** (except for confidentiality and exclusivity clauses), but it shows serious intent and outlines key deal terms.

KEY COMPONENTS OF AN LOI

1. PURCHASE PRICE

- Total consideration being offered
- Example: $4,400,000

2. FORM OF TRANSCATION

- Stock purchase vs. asset purchase
- What's included and excluded

3. PAYMENT TERMS

- Cash at closing: $3,900,000
- Seller note: $500,000 (5 years, 6% interest, interest-only with balloon payment)

4. FINANCING CONTINGENCY

- Buyer must secure SBA or conventional financing

5. DUE DILLIGENCE PERIOD

- Typically 30-45 days from execution of LOI
- Buyer has right to terminate or renegotiate price and/or terms if due diligence reveals problems

6. EXLUSIVITY PERIOD

- Seller agrees not to entertain other offers during due diligence
- Usually matches the DD period

7. SELLER TRANSITION/CONSULTING

- Seller stays on for 3-12 months
- Compensation and hours specified

8. NON-COMPETE AGREEMENT

- Duration (typically 3-5 years)
- Geographic scope
- Industry restrictions

9. BUILDING LEASE (IF APPLICABLE)

- If seller owns the building, lease terms
- Duration should exceed loan term

10. CONDITIONS TO CLOSING

- Clean due diligence
- No material adverse changes
- Financing approval

- Key employee retention

WHY LOIs MATTER

The LOI accomplishes several things:

1. **Gets both parties aligned** on major terms before spending money on lawyers, CPA's or travel and operational audits.

2. **Takes the business off market** during your due diligence (exclusivity)

3. **Establishes timeline** for the transaction

4. **Protects confidentiality** of information exchanged

Once the LOI is signed, we move into due diligence. This is where the real work begins.

As a small note, you can gain access to an editable LOI Template through the link in the Resources section at the end of the book.

STEP 8: FINANCIAL DUE DILLIGENCE

Purpose: Confirm that the financial statements accurately represent the business and there are no hidden financial issues.

What we're looking for:

- Accuracy of reported EBITDA

- Quality of earnings (are revenues sustainable?)

- Working capital requirements

- Inventory accuracy (can swing valuations by 10-20%)
- Hidden liabilities
- Revenue concentration (are they dependent on one customer?)
- Seasonality and trends

Additional documents we request:

- 3-5 years of profit & loss statements
- 3-5 years of balance sheets
- 3-5 years of tax returns
- Bank statements (last 12-24 months)
- General ledger
- Accounts receivable aging report
- Accounts payable aging report
- Work in progress (WIP) reports
- Customer revenue analysis
- Inventory records with valuation methodology
- Debt schedules
- CapEx history and plans

Additional red flags we look for:

- Declining revenues or profit margins

- Accounting irregularities
- Mismatched tax returns vs. P&L statements
- Excessive owner discretionary expenses
- Unpaid payroll taxes (this can kill a deal instantly)
- Inventory discrepancies

Quality of Earnings (QOE) Analysis:

For larger deals ($5M+), we conduct a formal QOE. This is like a mini-audit that validates:

- Revenue recognition is appropriate
- Expenses are accurately categorized
- One-time expenses vs. recurring expenses
- Adjusted EBITDA calculations are correct
- Working capital is normalized

This analysis typically costs between $15,000-$50,000, depending on business size.

Worth every penny. We've walked away from deals after QOE revealed the real EBITDA was 30-40% lower than advertised.

Timeline: 2-3 weeks typically

STEP 9: LEGAL DUE DILLIGENCE

Purpose: Identify any legal risks, pending litigation, contract issues, or compliance problems that could create liabilities post-acquisition.

What We're Reviewing:

Corporate & Organizational:

What we need to know about Corporate & Organizational:

1. Are there any legal issues or pending legal issues that may arise?

2. Can we verify the business entity from a legal standpoint? Ensure that it is an active corporation.

3. Ensure all licenses required to operate the business are active and there will be no renewals that will be required that are not covered by current staff.

Required information from Seller:

- Articles of Incorporation
- Operating Agreement
- Shareholder agreements
- Board meeting minutes (3-5 years)
- List of all shareholders and ownership percentages
- Business licenses and permits
- DBA registrations

- Organizational chart

Contracts & Agreements:

What we need to know about contracts:

1. Will the contracts be assignable to a new Owner?

2. Is there a transfer fee?

3. Are there any contract terms, licensing or distribution rights that change upon ownership change?

4. What happens to the business if a specific contract ends and is there a back up supplier/vendor?

5. What are the contract renewal terms when they expire?

Required Information from Seller:

- Customer contracts (all active + expired within last 3 years)
- Supplier and vendor agreements
- Franchise or distribution agreements
- Employment agreements
- Non-compete and confidentiality agreements
- Warranty or service agreements
- Any government contracts

Real Estate:

What we need to know from Real Estate, if leasing:

1. What are the lease terms and renewal options?
2. Ensure it is transferrable to a new owner.
3. What are the actual costs for the lease? If NNN, ensure you understand the total costs.
4. Is there a possibility to negotiate new more favorable lease terms?
5. Check how other tenants feel about the landlord, if applicable.
6. Does the landlord respond quickly to issues?
7. Ensure the business is being operated within the city/county zoning guidelines for that type of property.

Required Information from Seller:

- Property leases (critical—we need lease terms that extend beyond our loan term)
- Deeds and titles if they own property
- Zoning compliance
- Environmental reports (Phase I/II)
- Any liens or encumbrances

Intellectual Property:

What we need to know for IP:

1. Ensure that no other companies exist that could threaten your trademarks.

2. If the company relies on unique specialized technology, ensure that a solid copyright or patent is in place to protect the IP from competitors being able to steal.

3. Verify that the seller owns the domains and not someone else. (we have seen this)

Required Information from Seller:

- Trademarks and service marks
- Patents and copyrights
- Domain names
- Software licenses
- IP litigation history

Employment & Benefits:

- Employee roster with compensation
- Employee handbook
- Benefit plans
- Union or collective bargaining agreements
- Independent contractor agreements
- Any employment disputes or claims
- I-9 forms and compliance documents

Litigation & Disputes:

- All pending or threatened litigation (last 5 years)
- Settlement agreements
- Insurance claims history

Insurance:

- All current policies
- Coverage amounts
- Loss runs (3-5 years)

Regulatory & Compliance:

- Licenses and permits required
- Correspondence with regulatory agencies
- Inspection reports
- Compliance policies

CRITICAL PROVISIONS WE LOOK FOR

One of the most important things we check are **change of control provisions**.

Some contracts include clauses that say if the business is sold, the contract must be renegotiated. This can be devastating.

Example: The business has a contract with a major supplier who gives them materials at $1.00 per unit. A great price, but there's a change of control clause...and after you buy the business, the supplier says, "We want $1.50 per unit now."

That 50% increase can destroy margins overnight.

We review every significant contract for:

- Change of control provisions
- Assignment restrictions
- Termination rights
- Automatic renewals
- Price escalation clauses

Timeline: 2-3 weeks typically

STEP 10: OPERATIONAL DUE DILLIGENCE

Purpose: Understand how the business operates day-to-day, identify inefficiencies, assess key person dependency risk, and uncover opportunities for improvement.

What we're evaluating:

Operations & Systems:

- Standard Operating Procedures (SOPs)
- Quality control processes
- Production/service delivery workflows
- Technology systems and software

- Equipment condition and maintenance records
- Facility conditions
- Supply chain and vendor relationships

Sales & Marketing:

- Marketing plan and budget
- Lead generation systems
- Sales process and conversion rates
- Customer acquisition cost (CAC)
- Lifetime value (LTV) of customers
- Marketing materials and campaigns
- Website and digital presence
- Sales team structure and compensation

Customers:

- Customer satisfaction scores
- Customer retention rates
- Concentration analysis
- Revenue by customer segment
- Contract terms and renewal rates
- Growth opportunities

Employees:

What we need to know from Employment & Benefits:

1. Have there been any compensation increases/benefits promised to any employees? If so, what are they?
2. How does the pay of the current employees compare to industry benchmarks in this area and that of competitors?
3. Have there been any labor disputes and are there any current labor disputes?
4. Who are the KEY employees and does the Seller have "Key Man" insurance policies?
5. What is the employee sentiment around the sale of the business, if they are aware?
6. Are there any "at-risk" employees that have a higher chance of leaving when the business is sold?
7. Meet with the current/past owner and review what he/she feels about each employee. Employee happiness, engagement, performance level.
8. Have we lost any employees in the past 12 months? If so, review each situation. Where did they go? Why did they leave?
9. Are there any problem employees? If yes, what's wrong?
10. Who are the star employees and why?

Required Information from Seller:

- Key employee dependencies
- Skills and certifications
- Compensation relative to market
- Culture and morale
- Turnover rates
- Succession planning

Competition:

- Competitive landscape
- Market share
- Competitive advantages/disadvantages
- Barriers to entry in the market

Growth & Scalability:

- Strategic growth plans
- Capital requirements for growth
- Constraints (talent, technology, capital, facility space)
- Market opportunity size

KEY PERSON RISK ASSESSMENT

This is critical. We need to know:

- Can this business run without the current owner?
- Which employees are critical to operations?
- What knowledge transfer needs to happen?
- Are customer relationships owner-dependent?
- Is there a "Keyman" insurance policy in place?

If the owner *is* the business, we need a detailed transition plan. Minimum 3-6 months.

Red flags in operational DD:

- Few documented processes (Most knowledge is in people's heads)
- High customer concentration
- Outdated technology
- Deferred maintenance on equipment
- Key employees planning to leave
- Owner working 60+ hours/week in the business
- No marketing systems (100% referral-based)

Timeline: 2-3 weeks, often overlapping with financial and legal DD

How To Save Time

Doing everything alone means you have to take this entire process step by step. If neither you nor the owner are in a rush, and if you enjoy this entire DD Process, then that's definitely an option.

In most of our cases, we don't have the luxury of taking 2-3 months just for DD. So we tend to run the three processes (Financial, Legal, and Operational) in parallel.

Either way, we have senior specialists with minimum 10 years experience in each area, and they're used to working as a team. So instead of 6-12 weeks, we can get all DD done in under a month.

The most important detail to keep in mind is that DD can go either way. You might conclude the business is great! Or that several things are wrong with it, and it's not worth pursuing.

Or just that you need to renegotiate a lower price and/or better terms. In any case, it matters if you spent 2-3 *months* reviewing this one deal, or 2-3 *weeks*.

STEP 11: PREPARE SBA LENDER PACKAGE

After due diligence, we prepare a comprehensive package for the SBA lender.

Most buyers submit terrible packages and get denied. We've perfected this process.

ITEMS INCLUDED IN EVERY PACKAGE:

1. PROFESSIONAL COVER LETTER

A 2-3 page letter outlining:

- Buyer's strengths and experience
- Business strengths and market position
- Growth opportunity
- Why this is a strong lending opportunity

2. EXECUTIVE SUMMARY

One-page overview of the deal with key highlights.

3. COMPREHENSIVE BUSINESS PLAN (20-30 PAGES)

This is where amateur buyers fail. It's all about risk. The goal is to show the lender and the SBA that *there will be minimal risk* with this transaction. SBA requires a detailed business plan with each loan application, but most people submit a hodge podge of information that does not inspire the confidence the SBA needs to feel their investment is safe.

That's why the SBA has developed a reputation as being overly picky with loan approvals.

But that does not need to be the case. Our team has gotten dozens of SBA loans approved over the years, so we can tell you from first hand experience that it can be done.

Here's what lenders actually look for in a business plan:

- Executive Summary
- Company Overview & history

- Market Analysis
- Competitive Analysis
- Management Team Bios
- Detailed Growth Strategy
- Marketing & Sales Plan
- Operations Plan
- Financial Projections (3-5 Years)
- Risk Analysis & Mitigation Strategies
- Use of Proceeds

4. FINANCIAL PROJECTIONS

Detailed 3-year projections showing:

- Revenue growth assumptions (conservative)
- Margin improvement plans
- Cost structure optimization
- Cash flow projections
- Break-even analysis
- Sensitivity analysis

5. PERSONAL FINANCIAL STATEMENT

Complete disclosure of buyer's personal assets, liabilities, income.

6. CREDIT REPORT & EXPLANATION

If there are any credit issues, we explain them proactively.

7. INDUSTRY RESEARCH

Third-party data showing industry trends, growth rates, market size.

8. SUPPORTING DOCUMENTS

- Purchase agreement or LOI
- Business tax returns
- Business financial statements
- QOE report (if conducted)
- Equipment lists and valuations
- Lease agreements
- Key customer/vendor contracts

THE GOAL

When the SBA underwriter opens this package, we want them to say, "Wow, this is professional. This deal is solid. Approved."

Most of the time, that's exactly what happens.

Cost to prepare: $5,000-$10,000 in professional services.

Success rate when properly prepared: 90%+

WHY THIS MATTERS

SBA is very cautious about approvals. They're protecting taxpayer money through their guarantee program. They want to see:

1. **The business is healthy** and can easily support the debt
2. **The buyer is qualified** with relevant experience and strong financials
3. **The deal structure makes sense** and is appropriately priced
4. **There's a growth plan** that's realistic and achievable

When you give them all of this in a professional, organized package, approval becomes straightforward.

If you'd like any assistance with preparing a lender package that has the highest chances of getting approved, reach out to our team using the email in the Resources section at the end of the book.

STEP 12: FINALIZE PURCHASE AND SALE AGREEMENTS

Once the lender gives approval, you finalize the legal documents.

WHAT YOU'RE ACTUALLY SELLING

During the M&A Process, you should be signing multiple documents. Here's what each one means:

1. CONFIDENTIALITY AGREEMENT

Protects the seller's confidential information during due diligence. Standard. Always sign this before seeing financial details.

2. LETTER OF INTENT (LOI)

Already covered earlier.

3. PURCHASE & SALE AGREEMENT (PSA)

This is one of *the* binding contracts. Usually 40-80 pages. Covers:

- Purchase price and payment terms
- Assets/stock being purchased
- Representations and warranties
- Indemnification provisions
- Closing conditions
- Post-closing covenants

Your attorney should review this carefully.

4. SELLER FINANCING NOTE

If the seller is providing financing, this document outlines:

- Loan amount
- Interest rate

- Payment terms
- Security interest
- Default provisions

5. EMPLOYMENT/CONSULTING AGREEMENT

Most deals include a transition period where the seller stays on to train the buyer and/or their team. This agreement specifies:

- Duration (usually 3-12 months)
- Compensation
- Responsibilities
- Hours per week

6. NON-COMPETE AGREEMENT

Prevents the seller from starting a competing business. Usually:

- 3-5 year term
- Geographic restriction (reasonable radius)
- Industry-specific

7. LEASE ASSIGNMENT OR NEW LEASE

If the business operates from a leased space, the buyer needs:

- Landlord approval of assignment

- Or a new lease in the buyers name
- Terms should extend beyond your loan term

8. BILL OF SALE

Transfers ownership of assets from seller to buyer.

9. ASSIGNMENT & ASSUMPTION AGREEMENTS

Transfers contracts, leases, licenses, etc. from seller to buyer.

CRITICAL PROVISIONS TO NEGOTIATE

Representations & Warranties:

The seller represents that:

- Financial statements are accurate
- There are no undisclosed liabilities
- There are no pending litigations
- All assets are in good working order
- Customer relationships are transferable

Indemnification:

If something the seller represented turns out to be false, they're liable.

We typically negotiate:

- 12-24 month indemnification period

- Seller holds back 10-15% of purchase price in escrow
- Released after indemnification period expires

Earnouts:

If there's disagreement on value, an earnout ties part of the purchase price to future performance.

As an example, let's say an offer is made on a business for $7M, but the current owner predicts industry shifts in their favor, potentially doubling the business, and so they're asking for $8M.

In this case, an Earnout term can be added, whereby if the company doubles in EBITDA within 2 years, the seller is paid an additional $1M.

STEP 13: CLOSE THE DEAL

Closing day is the culmination of months of work. Here's what happens:

The Closing Process:

1. **Final walkthrough** - Verify condition of assets, inventory count
2. **Wire transfer** - Buyer's cash goes into escrow
3. **Lender funding** - SBA loan funds transfer
4. **Document signing** - All parties sign the mountain of paperwork
5. **Keys and access** - You receive keys, passwords, access to systems
6. **Announcement** - Communicate (or schedule the communication of) transition to employees, customers, vendors

What You Need to Bring:

- Cashier's check or wire transfer for your down payment
- Valid ID
- Any final documents attorneys request

Timeline:

Closing typically takes 2-4 hours with all parties present (or via electronic signing).

What Happens After Closing:

- The buyer now owns the business (congratulations!)
- The seller has funds landing in their account (congratulations!)
- Transition period begins
- Seller starts training the buyer and/or their team
- Buyer's team starts implementing your 100-day plan
- Robert's automation systems kick in (Chapter 12)

COMMON MISTAKES TO AVOID

After overseeing over $200Million in business transactions, from both sides, we've seen probably every mistake imaginable. Here are the big ones:

1. No Clear Exit Strategy

As a buyer, don't buy random businesses. Have a plan. (As we discussed earlier in this chapter.)

As a seller, think: If the deal goes through, how will I invest the cash, so I can leverage the sale to attain more wealth?

2. Overpaying / Underselling

Emotion kills deals. Stick to factual valuations.

3. Skipping Due Diligence

"Trust but verify" isn't paranoia—it's prudence. For both sides.

4. Poor Deal Structure

Price matters less than terms. Master deal structuring.

5. Assuming You Can Fix Everything

As a buyer, buy businesses that work NOW. Don't buy projects.

As a seller, realize that buyers don't see your business with your eyes...they see it through 3rd party eyes.

So the simplest thing you can do to improve your business is to hire a 3rd party team to come in and assess (and maybe even improve) everything for you.

We like to remind ourselves of the maxim: "Sweat more in training, bleed less in war."

6. Ignoring Key Person Risk

As a buyer, know that if the business can't run without the owner, you're buying a job.

As a seller, the more of your responsibilities you can delegate to a competent team, the higher your take home will be in a sale.

7. Inadequate Working Capital

Always have 6-12 months of operating reserves. This is true for both sides.

8. No Growth Plan

SBA wants to see how you, as the new owner, will grow the business. So should you.

9. Weak Lender Package

This kills more deals than anything else. Invest in a professional package.

10. Moving Too Fast

Good deals take 5-12 months from first contact to closing. Don't rush.

ACTION STEPS

Now it's time to act. Here's your roadmap:

1. **Decide your acquisition strategy.** Buy-and-hold for cash flow, or roll-up for windfall exit? Write it down this week.

2. **Define your buy box.** Complete the buy box template. Be specific about industry, size, geography, and criteria.

3. **Build your acquisition team.** At minimum, you need: An M&A advisor, a CPA familiar with business acquisitions, an M&A attorney, and an SBA lender relationship. Start making these connections now.

4. **Research SBA loan requirements.** Visit sba.gov or speak with an SBA lender to understand the process and requirements.

5. **Calculate your buying power.** Based on your current assets and

down payment capacity, what size businesses can you afford? Use the 10% and 5% down strategies to map out possibilities.

6. **Research deal sourcing strategies.** Learn about omnipresent marketing approaches including email, direct mail, phone outreach, and LinkedIn. Consider which channels make most sense for your target market.

7. **Consider working with an M&A advisor.** The deal sourcing, valuation, and structuring process requires expertise. Partners can help you navigate off-market deals and complex negotiations.

8. **Understand the key lender metrics.** Calculate the DSCR for any business you're evaluating. If it's below 1.5, you'll have financing challenges. Above 2.0 is ideal.

Of course, if you'd like support with any part of the above, you can reach out to our team using the email in the Resources section of the book, and we'll help as much as we can.

You now have the complete roadmap for acquiring cash-flowing businesses that double your net worth, year after year.

The question isn't whether this works. The math proves it works.

The question is: *Will* you do (or outsource) the work?

In the next chapter, Robert will show you exactly how to systematize and automate these businesses so they run without you—allowing you to scale to multiple acquisitions and build true generational wealth.

Let's go.

CHAPTER 12

AUTOMATE

You've acquired a business. (Or you've decided to sell your business.) Now what?

Most people think the hard part is over once they close the deal. The reality? That's when the real work begins.

Robert co-wrote an entire book on this subject. It's called *Unshackled: The 7 Levels of Business Excellence*. Nearly 250 pages of strategies, insights, and tools on how to build a business that operates 100% without you. If you want the complete system, we recommend reading it.

But in this chapter, we're going to give you the highlights. The most fundamental parts. The strategies you can act on immediately to see ROI from these efforts.

Because here's the truth: if you can't automate your business, you don't own a business. You have a glorified job. And probably an expensive, stressful one.

The goal of this chapter is simple: show you how to improve and systematize your operations. So you can acquire multiple businesses. So you can scale. So you can actually build wealth instead of just trading time for money.

We'll break this down into four key areas:

1. Document Operations

2. Empower Everyone

3. Define Culture

4. Constant Improvement

Ready? Let's get started.

DOCUMENT OPERATIONS

Almost every business book in history talks about the importance of having everything written down and clearly defined.

And yet, the vast majority of businesses either don't have their operations documented, or they have documentation that nobody actually uses. Half-defined processes that people (maybe) follow halfway through.

Why?

Because most people approach documentation backwards. They try to write SOPs in isolation, without input from the people who actually do the work.

Here's how to do it right.

STEP 1: CONDUCT INTERVIEWS

Before you write a single procedure, talk to the people affected by it.

If you're building a sales process, interview your sales team. Interview clients you've successfully sold to. Interview prospects you've lost. Get their perspective on what works and what doesn't.

If you're documenting customer service, talk to your customer service reps. Talk to customers. Understand where the friction points are.

The goal isn't to create some theoretical perfect process. The goal is to capture what *actually* works in the real world and make it *repeatable*.

STEP 2: TAKE DETAILED NOTES

This is critical: take *detailed* notes, not summaries.

When someone explains how they handle a customer complaint, don't write "resolve customer issues promptly." That's useless.

Instead, write: "When a customer emails with a complaint, acknowledge receipt within 30 minutes. Ask three clarifying questions: What happened? What were you expecting? What would make this right? Then escalate to a manager if the refund exceeds $500."

See the difference? One is a generality. The other is specific, and as such... *actionable*.

Just for clarity, the actual SOPs we write are much more detailed than the above, but even the above example highlights how important it is to give people *all* the details they need to (a) understand what "good work" looks like, and (b) how to actually get it done, at a high standard, every time.

STEP 3: CENTRALIZE EVERYTHING

All of your documentation needs to live in one place where everyone can access it.

We use Alvanda.com for our operational documentation. Other companies use Notion, Confluence, or custom wikis. The tool doesn't matter. What matters is:

- Everyone knows where to find it

- It's searchable
- It's kept up to date
- It's organized logically

Dead documentation is worse than no documentation. If your team doesn't use it, you wasted your time creating it.

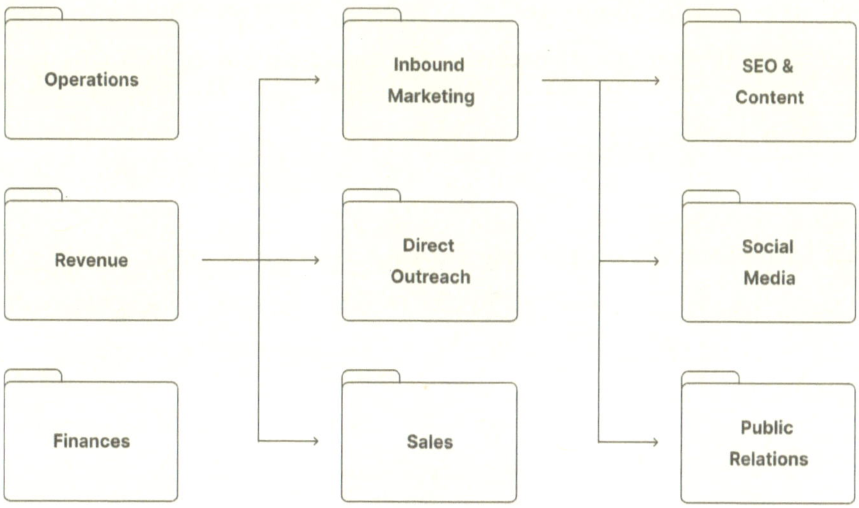

Graphic: Organized Documentation.

THE DOCUMENTATION TEST

Here's how you know if your documentation is good enough:

Could you hire someone tomorrow, hand them your documentation, and have them successfully complete the task without asking you a single question?

If the answer is no, your documentation needs work.

The standard we hold ourselves to at Elkridge Advisors is this: any new team member should be able to reference our documentation and execute

80% of their role within their first week. The other 20% they'll learn through experience.

That's the level of clarity you're aiming for.

EMPOWER EVERYONE

One of the main reasons most business owners are unable to detach themselves from their operations is because they do not sufficiently empower their staff—or because they didn't use the right methods of empowerment.

One is typically a lack of willingness. The other is lack of competence.

In both cases, the outcome is the same: you as the owner or general manager have to be involved in day-to-day operations. Otherwise, the business won't function as well as it could without you being there.

We've found many tools that help with this, but here are the top three.

1. PROFESSIONAL DEVELOPMENT PLANS

PDPs are two-way conversations between Managers and their direct reports.

If you have layers of management, every manager should do this with their direct reports. C-level speaks to middle management, middle management speaks to their direct reports. And so on.

Even if you have a non-hierarchical company, you should still implement PDPs. If you have 50 employees, you probably can't do PDPs with all 50. You should do PDPs with your top 5-10 people, and then they do PDPs with their teams.

Frequency:

- When someone's new or when you're just starting PDPs: **weekly**
- Once established: **monthly**

The PDP Framework:

These are structured conversations where you provide or get feedback on day-to-day operations. Here's the format:

1. **Current Reality** – What's actually happening right now?
2. **Expected Reality** – What should be happening?
3. **Action Plan** – What will the person do about it?
4. **Support Needed** – Do they need any support to achieve the outcome?
5. **Timeline** – By when will this outcome be achieved?
6. **Follow-up Notes** – Was it successful? What happened?

Example: Being Late to Meetings

Let's say someone tends to be late for calls.

You start the PDP conversation:

Current Reality: What's actually happening right now?

"You are sometimes late for calls."

Expected Reality: What should be happening?

"You're always on time for calls. When you're late, it's a very rare occurrence—maybe once every two months. But generally, when calls start, you're already there."

Action Plan: "What are you going to do about it?"

The person might say: "I don't know what to do because I already set alarms for myself."

You dig deeper: "Show me your alarms. We had a 10 AM meeting yesterday. Show me the alarm you set for that."

They show you. The alarm is set for 10:00 AM.

You point out: "You had a 10 AM meeting. Why was your alarm at 10 AM? Why wasn't it at 9:55? You need your alarm to sound *before* the meeting if you want to make the meeting on time."

This seems obvious to someone who's always punctual, but people who aren't punctual can make such rookie mistakes.

Support Needed: "Do you need any support from me on this?"

In this case, probably nothing. They can just change their alarms themselves. In other cases, they might need access to specific tools, or they might want coaching from a senior. Every case is different. What's important is that *if* someone needs help, we find a way to get it.

Timeline: By when will this outcome be achieved?

"One week from now, we will check in to see if we're on time for all meetings these next few days."

Follow-up: One week later, you review. Were they on time? Yes or no. Document the result. Leave this PDP there, set in stone. What happened, happened.

If they're still late, create another PDP. "You are STILL late for meetings..." Etc. And this time come up with another solution. The next plan might be slightly different or completely different.

Of course, if someone simply does not improve, you always have the option of firing them. However, having several weeks or months of PDPs, where they clearly failed to meet expectations, makes the decision much clearer because you tried, multiple times, and no one can contradict you.

Even from a legal standpoint, the company is much better off, because if an employee ever wants to "fight against" being let go, then you have weeks or months of documentation to prove your decision. And if you use something like Alvanda, all those inputs are timestamped, with the exact date, time, and participants of the PDP.

If you'd like an editable PDP Template, you can gain access to one through the link in the Resources section at the end of the book.

2. LEAD AND LAG MEASURES

Most people don't understand this distinction because they don't understand how business and life work.

The vast majority of businesses—over 90%, probably closer to 95%—only have **lag measures**. They only track outcomes:

- Number of clients closed
- Revenue in the door
- Profit margin
- Number of new customers

These are **lag measures** because they lag behind the actions that created them. You need to perform certain activities for a lag measure to occur.

If the only types of measures you have are lagging KPIs, you can lose sight of what you actually need *to do* to reach those outcomes.

We're not saying you shouldn't have lag measures. You absolutely should. But for every lag measure, you should have at least one lead measure of what you're going to act on so you *reach* that lag measure.

Example: New Clients

Let's say your lag measure is "number of new clients."

Some **lead measures** could be:

- # of emails sent
- # Minutes to reply to an email
- # of Initial Calls made
- # of followup Calls IF no answer

These are just examples. There can be many more.

Why This Matters:

We're not adding 20 KPIs to complicate your life. We're adding these KPIs to **simplify** your life.

Right now, if your only measure is "number of clients," you don't know just by looking where the funnel is breaking down. You might think you just need to send more emails.

But if you look at the lead measures, you might see:

- You're sending 10,000 emails
- Your open rate is 1%
- That means 9,900 emails are never being seen
- Only 100 emails are actually reaching prospects
- Your entire pipeline is based on those 100 emails

Obviously, your issue isn't the number of emails you're sending. Your issue is getting those emails into your ideal clients' inboxes.

If you have these lead measures set up, you'll know where the problem is immediately. You'll realize: "This shouldn't be the case. We're doing something wrong. We're either being marked as spam, or the tool we're using isn't working, or our domain is unhealthy."

The conclusions you'll reach—you'll reach them faster, and you'll reach better conclusions because you implemented lead measures.

Note on lag measures: We probably don't need to explain lag measures extensively because almost everyone already sets them. We want to make this book as short and useful as possible.

3. SCOREBOARDS

Now that you have lead measures and lag measures—the ones you want to focus on this month or this quarter—we go onto **Scoreboards**.

Scoreboards are typically for a team. The sales team has a Scoreboard. The marketing team has one. Service delivery, IT, HR, everyone.

Even if it's a one-person team—even if your entire sales department is one person—that one person should have a Scoreboard specifically for them.

Why Scoreboards?

If you go to a basketball game and you're watching the game but there's no scoreboard, you don't know how many hoops one team scored versus the other. You don't know how many fouls there are. You're just guessing who's winning, for the entire game.

Very few people would be able to keep track correctly of everything that's going on.

That's why you have a scoreboard. It's visual. It's big. Everyone sees it. Everyone knows: Where am I winning? Where am I losing? And based on that information, I can make better decisions.

Scoreboard Elements:

1. **The KPIs being measured**
2. **The expected outcome of that KPI**
3. **The total cumulative/average** (a sum or average of the period being measured—automatically calculated)
4. **Daily/weekly/monthly results** (you add the actual results here)

Measure	Target	Actual	W1	W2	W3
Response Time	<30Min	54Min	92Min	44Min	27Min
Resolution Time	<24Hrs	41Hrs	73Hrs	27Hrs	22Hrs
Win/Loss			**Loss**	**Loss**	**Win**

Graphic: Scoreboard Example.

Example: Customer Support Scoreboard

Let's say we have two KPIs for customer support:

KPI #1: Response Time

- **Expected Outcome:** Under 30 minutes during business hours

KPI #2: Resolution Time

- **Expected Outcome:** Under 24 hours (from the time a clients reports a problem until it's fixed)

Then you have the formula that calculates the averages in both cases.

Then you have columns for each week (or day, depending on your measurement frequency).

In this case, how can we measure?

If you don't have automatic systems, then what you can do is every week, you go into your inbox and measure response time.

If you have 10 total client inquiries, look at each one. If you have a thousand client inquiries because you're a big business, randomly look at 10. Pick two per day randomly.

Then measure response time and resolution time for those same inquiries. Get the average.

Let's say the average for last week was:

- **Response time:** 2 hours
- **Resolution time:** 2 days

Now you have data. The scoreboard is telling the team: **Are we winning or are we losing?**

Then you have conversations.

"Why is it taking so long for us to reply? This is our job. This is our main thing—promptness of replies and promptness of solutions."

Some might be excuses, but they're still reasons.

Then you ask: **"What do we need to do differently? How can we improve our performance in these areas?**

Every single week, you can now have these productive conversations *because* there's a scoreboard, showing everyone exactly how we're progressing from one day or week to the next.

The result of implementing these three tools:

When you use PDPs, lead/lag measures, and Scoreboards together, your team can reach a level of empowerment way beyond that of most businesses. They know what's expected. They know how they're performing. They know what to improve.

And you? You're no longer trapped in day-to-day operations. You've started building a system that runs without you.

DEFINE CULTURE

After you've documented your operations and started empowering your team, it's time to define your culture.

This is the third step in the automation process, and it's critical. Culture is what holds everything together when you're not in the room.

These steps are presented in the order we expect you to implement them as soon as you read this book. Number one: document operations through interviews. Number two: start empowering your team. Number three: define your culture.

By the time you get here, you've already started implementing the first two steps. You have a good pulse on what's going on in your business because you've been interviewing people and empowering them through PDPs, lead/lag measures, and Scoreboards.

Now you're ready to formalize your culture.

STEP 1: DEFINE YOUR VISION

The vision is a **one-page narrative snapshot** of one day in the future, three to five years from now.

For example, someone reading this book in 2026, might set their vision for 2030.

Here's how to create it:

Choose a specific date. Pick an actual date on the calendar. Robert always uses his birthday. So he'll say, "It's December 5th, 2030" (or whatever year is three to five years out for you).

Describe the business on that day—in the present tense.

Write as if you're living that day right now. Don't talk about how you got there. Don't talk about what you're going to do after. Just describe what *is* on that specific day.

Include details like:

- How much money are we making?
- How many clients do we have?
- What's our profit margin?

- What services are we rendering?
- How are we rendering those services?
- What critical departments exist in the business?
- What are those departments doing?
- What do our sales efforts look like?
- What do our marketing efforts look like?

Length: Between half a page to one full page. Not shorter than half a page. Not longer than one page.

This is your destination. You know where Chicago is because you're there. But you need to know where New York is if you want to get there. Your vision is New York. The destination.

Once you define the vision, anyone in your business can look at it and understand: **This is where we're going.**

STEP 2: DEFINE YOUR MISSION STATEMENT

The mission statement is very short. **Just one sentence.** Intentionally one sentence—something you can remember and say very easily.

The mission statement guides all decisions in the company. The vision gives direction (where we're going), and the mission gives guidance on the way we'll get there.

For example, our mission statement at Elkridge Advisors is:

"To help ambitious individuals accelerate their wealth acquisition every year."

What does this tell us?

Who we work with: Ambitious individuals. If you're not ambitious, we're probably not a good fit.

What we do: We accelerate wealth acquisition. We're not assuming our clients don't already have a plan. We're assuming they do. They have some knowledge, some strategy they're implementing. What we do is we *accelerate* their wealth acquisition.

How we measure success: Every year. We help you accelerate your wealth more and more, year after year.

If you go the standard route—stocks or real estate—you typically get 8-12% per year. Very linear growth.

In our case, we add millions of dollars of net worth and passive income to our clients, every year. That's exponential growth. That's acceleration.

This feeds all our decisions:

- Whether we should work with an individual or not
- How we filter through deals
- How we think about timelines

It's not enough to grow someone's wealth. If they were already growing at 10% per year and we come in and they're still growing at 10% per year, we failed. We should be growing their wealth at 50% or 100% per year. That's how we know we've succeeded.

And if we grew someone's wealth by 50% in year one, but we don't manage to do that again in year two, again, we're not upholding our mission statement.

Your turn: Create a one-sentence mission statement for your business. Anyone in the business should be able to read it and determine whether any action they're taking is aligned with that mission or not.

STEP 3: DEFINE YOUR CORE VALUES

Core values are very personal. We're not going to prescribe what your core values should be. You need to define them based on what matters to you and your business.

Here are our three core values at Elkridge:

1. **Focus On Returns**
2. **Think Long-Term**
3. **Remain Friendly**

You can find descriptions of why we chose these three core values at elkridgeadvisors.com/company.

Your core values should reflect what you believe and how you operate. They should be genuine, not aspirational platitudes.

STEP 4: DGRAC ROLE DESCRIPTIONS

This is the final step in defining your culture.

DGRAC stands for:

- **D**esired Outcomes
- **G**uidelines
- **R**esources

- Accountability
- Consequences (for both success and failure)

If you correctly define every role in your company based on DGRAC role descriptions, and people follow those descriptions, **your business has a 100% chance of success.**

We're not saying 99%. We're saying **100%.**

If you've done everything up until now—documented operations, empowered your team, defined your vision, mission, and values—and then you create and follow DGRAC role descriptions, you will succeed. No exceptions.

Here's how DGRAC works, with examples:

D - Desired Outcomes

Why does this role exist? What is the result we expect from this role?

Example - CEO: The company generates more revenue and profit every quarter.

Example - Customer Success: All clients I'm responsible for are always well-informed, happy, and get the outcomes they want from our relationship.

G - Guidelines

Under guidelines, you put everything that would be useful for that person to know or do.

Example - CEO:

- Should have PDPs with all direct reports

- Should ensure we always have updated and relevant lead measures and lag measures
- Should implement new lead generation initiatives every quarter
- Should implement new profit improvement initiatives every quarter
- Etc.

Example - Customer Success:

- Should have notifications set up and always active on desktop or phone so they know immediately when a customer inquiry comes in
- Always check the Customer Success Library before answering questions. The latest versions of answers are always there.
- Etc.

R - Resources

What resources does this person have to do their job well?

Resources might include:

- Their inbox
- Software systems (we use Alvanda to manage our businesses—that's a resource everyone gets access to)
- Devices, like a phone or a video camera
- Transportation, like a car or public transport subscription

- Library of educational courses
- The Operation's Manual
- Etc.

A - Accountability

Here we define 3 things:

1. **Who are you accountable to?**
2. **How often are you accountable to them?**
3. **What are you accountable with?** (What metrics or deliverables?)

Example - CEO:

- Accountable to: Board of Directors
- How often: Once a month
- With what: Revenue this month, percentage of growth since last month, profit (dollar value) this month, percentage of profit growth since last month

In short, these four KPIs must be presented to the Board by the 5th of each month for the previous month.

Example - Customer Success:

- Accountable to: Director of Operations
- How often: Once a week

- With what: Average response time, Average time to solution, Number of new reviews or testimonials, Average rating on new reviews, Two ways to get more positive reviews next week.

C - Consequences (for Success and Failure)

Consequences for Success:

These are often obvious but shouldn't be taken for granted:

1. You get to keep your job
2. You get to be paid as agreed for the work you're rendering

Important note: If you're getting a salary, you're not being paid to exist. You're being paid to do good work—quality work, on-time. That's what we expect by default.

Additional consequences for overachieving:

Example: If we have over 10% revenue growth month-over-month while maintaining profit margin (or profit margin doesn't suffer more than 5%), you get a bonus of an additional 5% of your income that month.

Consequences for Failure:

Example - CEO with a negative month (revenue or profits go down):

- Provide a report explaining: (1) Why that happened, (2) What needs to be done to change it, (3) Action plan with firm, unmovable deadlines for implementing those changes.

Example - CEO with three consecutive negative months:

- Very high probability you will have to be let go.

The Power of DGRAC

When every role in your company has a clear DGRAC description, there's no ambiguity. Everyone knows:

- What success looks like
- What they need to do
- What resources they have
- Who they report to, on what, and how often
- What happens if they succeed or fail

This clarity is what allows your business to run without you. Culture isn't about ping-pong tables and free snacks. It's about clear expectations, aligned incentives, and accountability.

Define it properly, and your business becomes unstoppable.

If you'd like an editable DGRAC Role Description Template, you can gain access to one through the link in the Resources section at the end of the book.

CONSTANT IMPROVEMENT

If you've ever wondered what makes a company go from successful to industry-best, industry-leading, or even household-name status—it's this:

The principle of Kaizen—constant and never-ending improvement.

This is why Samsung is Samsung.. Why Google is a verb. And why Netflix is synonymous with movie streaming.

FROM SUCCESSFUL TO INDUSTRY-LEADING

Let's be clear: if you implement everything in this chapter up to this point—documenting operations, empowering your team, defining your culture—you will build a very successful company.

You'll be in the top 3-4% of businesses. For 95% of people, that's more than enough.

But this final stage—constant and never-ending improvement—is what you do if you want to take it one step above. If you want to get to a point where the name of your product becomes synonymous with your industry.

Examples of this level:

- **Kleenex** – It's not a Kleenex. It's a tissue. But people don't call it a tissue. They call it Kleenex because it's become synonymous with the product.
- **Netflix** – You don't say "watch a movie and chill." You say "Netflix and chill."
- **Google** – You don't say "search for it online." You say "Google it."
- **Pampers** – You say Pampers when you mean diapers—even if you're actually using Huggies. Imagine how ingrained that is. You don't even say "diapers" anymore. You say "Pampers."

That's the level constant improvement can take you to. Your company can become *the* name for the entire category.

HOW DO YOU GET THERE?

Here's the truth: you're already doing most of what's required if you've implemented the previous sections.

You already:

1. **Measure everything** – Through your lead measures, lag measures, and Scoreboards.

2. **Get feedback constantly** – From sales, marketing, customer support, internal operations through all the interviews you conduct.

3. **Make tweaks regularly** – Based on that feedback and data.

So why does this chapter exist? Why have a separate section if we've already talked about doing all of this?

Because some people simply stop.

They implement everything we've explained. They reach success—a level of success they desire. The owner gets comfortable. The team members get comfortable. Everyone has reached a level of success at which they're satisfied.

And then they stop improving.

This section exists to underline one critical fact:

If you want to always and consistently grow your company and your brand, you can never stop improving.

Even if something is already good, you ask the question: "How can we make this better?"

And you never stop asking that question.

That's it. That's the entire principle of constant improvement.

Keep measuring. Keep getting feedback. Keep making tweaks. Forever.

SHOULD EVERYONE DO THIS?

Here's our honest perspective:

No. Not everyone should pursue this level.

Everyone should strive towards a level of success they want. But not everyone needs to become a billion-dollar household name.

In Robert's exact words:

> "I don't want to be a billionaire. I've said this multiple times.
>
> If I can spend time with my children, enjoy my life, write books on the side—if I can do everything I want and still become a billionaire, okay, fine.
>
> I do everything I do to leave an impact and to build wealth for myself and others—to a sufficient level at which we're very happy and very comfortable.
>
> I will not sacrifice time with my children for money. That's a sacrifice I'm not willing to make.
>
> I will not wake up when my children are grown and regret that I wasn't there to experience their upbringing. I will not

be that guy.

And I will not be the guy who misses the upbringing of my grandchildren. Instead, I will be there as well.

I also avoid prioritizing money over time with my wife, my health, or any of my values.

So at one point, if we reach a sufficient level of success and everyone is happy, that's it. We can stay there. Yes, we can keep improving slightly, but not obsessively.

As an example from my life:

I have a business that's been generating seven figures in income—over a million dollars—every year for the past five years. And it's been cash flowing about a quarter million dollars per year, for five years straight.

Someone might say, 'Shouldn't it be growing?'

Sure, it *can* grow. It can double. It can even quadruple in a year. I almost know exactly what to do to make that happen.

However, I'm focused on other things. I'm not focused on that business. I'm very happy with where that business is, and it will keep making a quarter million in passive income for as long as I (or its next owner) will take good care of it.

And "take good care", for a business that's set up the way we teach you in this chapter, means about 1 hour of my time per week.

I'm very happy with that outcome."

ACTION STEPS

1. **Audit your current documentation.** What processes exist only in people's heads? Start with your three most critical business functions and document them this month.

2. **Implement PDPs.** Schedule monthly PDP meetings with your direct reports. Use the five-question framework: current reality, expected reality, action plan, support needed, timeline.

3. **Build at least one Scoreboard.** Choose your most important department or function. Define 2-3 KPIs, set expected outcomes, and start tracking and setting priorities with the team, weekly.

4. **Define your culture.** Write your vision statement, mission statement, and core values. Share them with your team and ask for feedback.

5. **Create one DGRAC role description.** Start with the role that's most critical to your business or causing the most confusion. Use it as a template for other roles.

6. **Pick one thing to improve this week.** Just one. Make it 5% better. Then do it again next week.

If you'd like assistance with any part of the Business Automation Process, reach out to our team using the email in the Resources section at the end of this book, and we'll get back to you swiftly.

PART III

CREATE GENERATIONAL WEALTH

"Your decisions from today forward will affect not only your life, but also your entire legacy."

— Dave Ramsey

Welcome to Part Three.

If you've completed Parts One and Two, you're no longer just building assets—you're operating a business portfolio. You've acquired (or own) at least one cash-flowing company. You've implemented Robert's automation systems so it runs without you. You're collecting passive income every month.

Congratulations. You're already doing what 99% of people never achieve.

Now comes the question that separates the comfortable from the hyper-wealthy:

Do you want to build an empire?

Part Three is where high net worth individuals become extraordinarily wealthy. This is where you don't just own a few assets—you build a portfolio worth tens of millions of dollars and engineer a windfall exit that creates generational wealth.

In Part One, you built your foundation—reaching $300,000 in assets.

In Part Two, you deployed that capital strategically—acquiring and/or systematizing cash-flowing businesses.

In Part Three, you'll execute the consolidation strategy that turns a few million in annual revenue into a $50-100 million exit to private equity.

Part Three is also split into two main sections:

CREATE EMPIRES

How to execute roll-up strategies, tuck-in acquisitions, and multiple arbitrage to build a portfolio.

EXIT WHEN THE TIME IS RIGHT

How to prepare for and execute a maximum-value sale to private equity or strategic buyers.

Together, these two strategies represent the culmination of everything you've learned in this book. They're how you take the businesses you've acquired and turn them into outstanding levels of wealth.

This is Patrick's domain. Over the past decade, he's helped clients build multi-million dollar portfolios through strategic acquisitions and roll-up strategies. He's seen which consolidation approaches work and which fail. He knows what private equity firms look for when they're writing eight- or even nine-figure checks.

One critical note before we begin: Building an empire isn't for everyone. If you're happy owning one or two businesses that generate $200K-$500K per year in passive income, that's completely valid. That's financial freedom. Enjoy it.

But if you want more—if you want to build something that makes you a deca-millionaire, that sets up your children and grandchildren—Part Three is your roadmap.

The math works. The strategies are proven. The only question is whether you desire to pursue this path.

If you are, then let's build an empire.

CHAPTER 13

CREATE EMPIRES

You've acquired your first business. Maybe your second. You've automated operations. The businesses are running. You're generating passive income.

Now what?

This is where most people stop. They own a few businesses, collect cash flow, and call it success.

And you know what? That IS success. If you get to this point, you're in the top 3% of entrepreneurs. You've built something most people never will.

But if you want to create generational wealth—the kind of wealth that changes your family's trajectory for the next century—you need to think bigger.

You need to create an empire.

This chapter is about scaling beyond a few businesses. It's about building a portfolio worth $50 million, $100 million, or more. It's about positioning yourself for a windfall exit that creates life-changing wealth in a single transaction.

THE PARADIGM SHIFT

Most business owners we talk to are completely consumed by internal operations.

They're hiring a new marketing person. They're worried about installing new equipment. They're managing day-to-day issues with clients, employees, and vendors.

They're so buried in the business that the idea of acquiring ANOTHER business sounds insane.

"I can barely breathe in my own business, Patrick. How am I supposed to acquire another one?"

We get it. That was the old paradigm.

Here's the new one:

You don't acquire businesses to work in them. You acquire businesses to consolidate them, systematize them, and multiply their value.

This is what private equity firms do every single day. This is how the ultra-wealthy build $100 million net worths in 10 years starting with a few million in capital.

And once you understand the mechanics of it, you'll never look at business acquisition the same way again.

This is how it works.

MULTIPLE ARBITRAGE

Everything in this chapter rests on one concept: multiple arbitrage.

Here's how it works:

Small businesses sell for 3-4X EBITDA.

If a business generates $1 million in EBITDA (earnings before interest, taxes, depreciation, and amortization), it's typically worth $3-4 million.

Larger businesses sell for 6-7X EBITDA or higher.

If a business generates $5 million in EBITDA, it's worth $30-35 million.

Same industry. Same type of business. The only difference is scale.

Why does the multiple increase?

Larger businesses are more valuable to buyers like private equity because they:

- Have more revenue stability
- Are less dependent on the owner
- Have better systems and processes
- Can support professional management teams
- Have more predictable cash flows
- Are easier to scale further

Now here's where it gets interesting.

Let's say you buy five plumbing companies. Each does $1 million in

EBITDA. Each costs $3 million (3X multiple).

Total investment: $15 million. Total EBITDA: $5 million.

Now you consolidate them under one brand. You eliminate redundancies. You implement Robert's automation systems from Chapter 12. You grow the combined entity by just 20% through better marketing and sales systems.

Now you have a company doing $6 million in EBITDA.

At a 6X multiple, that company is worth $36 million.

Again, you bought assets for $15 million...

They're now worth $36 million.

That's $21 million in value creation through multiple arbitrage alone—before any organic growth.

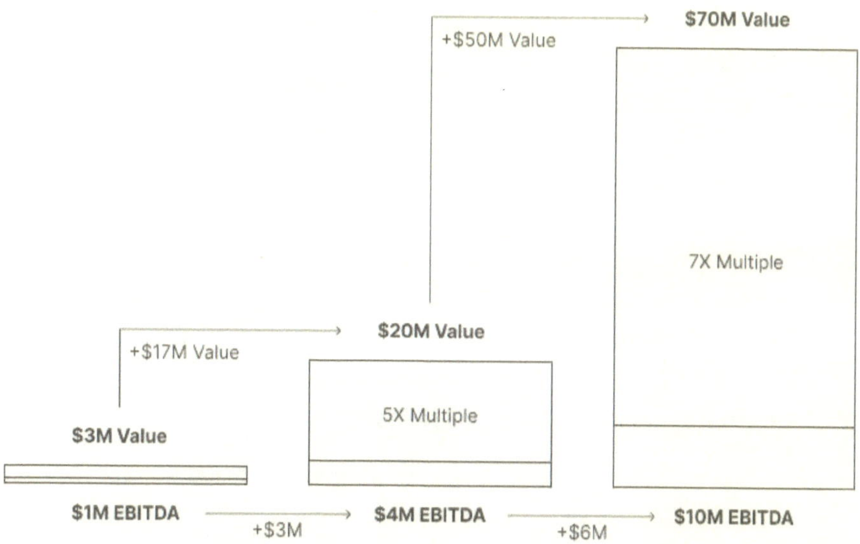

Graphic: Exponential Exit Multiples.

This is not theory. This happens every single week in M&A markets around the world.

And you cannot do this by buying random businesses.

You need a strategy. A consolidation thesis. A plan.

The following are several strategies for building an empire.

STRATEGY #1: THE ROLL-UP STRATEGY

A roll-up strategy is when you systematically acquire multiple businesses in the same industry with the explicit goal of consolidating them and selling to private equity for a windfall exit in 5-10 years.

Key elements of a successful roll-up:

1. PICK A FRAGMENTED INDUSTRY

You need an industry with hundreds or thousands of small operators. Industries dominated by a few large players won't work.

Great roll-up industries:

- Home services (plumbing, HVAC, electrical, roofing)
- Healthcare services (dental, med spas, physical therapy, veterinary)
- Professional services (accounting, insurance agencies, law firms)
- Facility services (janitorial, landscaping, pest control)
- Specialty manufacturing
- Regional distribution businesses

2. STAY FOCUSED ON ONE INDUSTRY

Don't buy a plumbing company, then a dental practice, then a landscaping business. That's not a roll-up. That's a random collection of businesses that nobody wants to buy.

Pick one industry. Become the expert. Dominate that niche.

IMPLEMENT COMMON BRANDING AND SOPs

As you acquire businesses, rebrand them under a common umbrella. Implement standardized processes. Create consistency across all locations.

This makes the business more valuable because it's less dependent on individual owners and more dependent on systems.

3. FOCUS ON ACQUISITION AND ORGANIC GROWTH

Don't just buy businesses and hope they grow. Most baby boomer businesses are referral-only with no formal marketing or sales systems.

Install marketing and sales systems. Turn on the "light switch" and drive new customer acquisition. Grow revenue 20-40% through better operations.

The combination of acquisition growth (buying more businesses) and organic growth (growing each business) creates exponential value.

THE MATH OF ROLL-UPS: A REAL EXAMPLE

Let's walk you through a real roll-up strategy so you can see exactly how the math works.

Starting Point:

You have a plumbing company in Baltimore doing $4 million in revenue and $800K in EBITDA. You bought it for $3.2 million (4X multiple) using SBA financing.

Year 1-2: Add Tuck-Ins

You acquire three smaller plumbing companies in the surrounding area:

- Company A: $200K EBITDA, purchased for $600K (3X)
- Company B: $300K EBITDA, purchased for $900K (3X)
- Company C: $250K EBITDA, purchased for $750K (3X)

Total spent on tuck-ins: $2.25 million. Combined EBITDA: $1.55 million ($800K + $200K + $300K + $250K).

Your enterprise is now doing $1.55 million in EBITDA.

Year 3-4: Install Systems and Grow

You implement Robert's automation systems from Chapter 12. You install formal marketing and sales systems. You grow organically by 25%.

New EBITDA: $1.94 million

Year 5: Add More Acquisitions

You acquire two more companies:

- Company D: $400K EBITDA, purchased for $1.2 million (3X)
- Company E: $500K EBITDA, purchased for $1.5 million (3X)

Combined EBITDA: $2.84 million ($1.94M + $400K + $500K)

Year 6-7: Final Growth Push

You optimize operations. You cross-sell services. You expand into new markets. You grow another 20%.

Final EBITDA: $3.4 million

Year 8: Exit to Private Equity

Your business is now doing $3.4 million in EBITDA. At a 7X multiple, it's worth approximately $24 million.

Your total investment:

- Platform company: $3.2M
- Tuck-ins and add-ons: $5.95M
- Total: $9.15M

Exit proceeds: $24 million

Value created: ~$15 million (before debt paydown, after-tax proceeds, etc.)

And here's the beautiful part: most of that $9.15M wasn't even your money. It was SBA loans, seller financing, and cash flow from the businesses themselves.

Your actual out-of-pocket cash might have been $1-2 million over 8 years.

That's how you turn $1-2 million into $15+ million in less than a decade.

THE PLATFORM ACQUISITION

Before you can do anything else, you need a platform company.

A platform company is your foundation. It's the larger, well-systemized business that everything else will be rolled into.

Platform company characteristics:

- $3-5 million in revenue minimum (ideally more)
- $500K-$1 million+ in EBITDA
- Has systems and processes in place
- Not completely owner-dependent
- Strong enough to absorb other businesses

Think of a platform company like a wheel. In a small business (under $2 million in revenue), the owner is the hub. Everything depends on them. Remove the owner, and the wheel falls apart.

In a platform company, the processes and systems are the hub. The owner can step away, and the business keeps running.

Why you need a platform first:

You cannot build a roll-up strategy on a tiny business. If you buy a $500K revenue company and start adding smaller companies to it, you're just creating a bigger mess.

Start with a strong platform. Then build around it.

TUCK-IN ACQUISITIONS

Once you have your platform, you start doing tuck-in acquisitions.

A tuck-in is when you buy a smaller business and immediately fold it into your platform company. You don't operate it separately. You absorb the clients, eliminate the redundant infrastructure, and instantly benefit from multiple arbitrage.

Here's a real example:

Let's say your platform company does $2 million in EBITDA at a 6X multiple. It's worth $12 million.

Now you find a small competitor doing $200K in EBITDA. At a small business multiple of 2-3X, you can buy it for $400K-$600K.

The moment you close the deal and tuck those clients into your platform company, your combined EBITDA becomes $2.2 million.

But here's the magic: those new clients aren't valued at a 2-3X multiple anymore. They're now part of your $12 million platform company that trades at 6X.

That $200K in EBITDA you just acquired is now worth $1.2 million in enterprise value (6X multiple).

You paid $400K. You created $1.2 million in value. That's an $800K gain literally overnight—on paper, through enterprise value.

Do that ten times, and you've created $8 million in enterprise value while spending $4 million on acquisitions.

This is how you build an empire.

ADD-ON ACQUISITIONS

Add-on acquisitions are similar to tuck-ins, but you keep them as separate operating entities under your parent company.

When to use add-ons instead of tuck-ins:

- The business is in a different geography that you want to expand into
- The business has a strong brand you don't want to eliminate
- There are operational reasons to keep it separate temporarily

Eventually, many add-ons become tuck-ins as you consolidate operations and branding. But initially, you might keep them separate for strategic reasons.

The multiple arbitrage still applies. You're still combining smaller businesses (bought at 3-4X) into a larger enterprise (valued at 6-7X).

BOLT-ON ACQUISITIONS

Bolt-on acquisitions are businesses in complementary or synergistic industries that create even more value when combined.

Example:

Let's say you own a commercial HVAC company. You're installing chillers at hospitals and office buildings.

Now you acquire a commercial plumbing company. They're also working on the same types of projects—hospitals and office buildings—just doing different work.

What happens when you combine them?

- Your HVAC clients now get introduced to plumbing services
- Your plumbing clients now get introduced to HVAC services
- You can bid on larger projects that require both trades
- You eliminate competition for overlapping clients
- You can create **hockey stick growth** from cross-selling

This is more than just multiple arbitrage. This is genuine synergy that creates value beyond the numbers.

Bolt-ons work best in industries where clients need multiple services—construction trades, professional services, healthcare services, facility management, etc.

STRATEGY #2: THE LADDER-UP STRATEGY

The ladder-up strategy is about progressively moving up the value chain as you build your empire.

How it works:

There's one more acquisition strategy we want to mention that can be a part of your play.

As opposed to a consolidation thesis, you do not need to focus on a single industry for the ladder up strategy. In a ladder up strategy, the whole premise is that a lender will qualify you for approximately the same size business as you own now, assuming you are running it well.

So, let's assume your first acquisition was a $5 million dollar garage installation company. Now, you purchase a second $5 million dollar business, let's say it is a pool maintenance company. You now own an aggregate of $10 million in annual revenue. Let's assume that both businesses are healthy well oiled machines and are producing a 20% profit margin.

A lender will qualify you to purchase a company for about the same annual revenue of business that you already own. So, instead of buying a third $5 million dollar business, you can now acquire a $10 million dollar business.

If you do, now you have $20 million in annual revenue. As such, on your next acquisition, you can purchase another $20 million company, and so on. Effectively doubling your portfolio, every year.

Many people think this is not realistic. Well... It is. In fact, buying a $20 million dollar business is a lot easier than buying a $3 million dollar business. Better books, better management talent, better strategies, better everything.

The only constraint, assuming your current businesses are run well and profitable, is the cash needed for injection. You can either stockpile profits as you grow and create a reserve for it, or get investors. And guess what? With our network, getting investors is easy when we prove our partners already have a proven history of running companies successfully.

The Ladder Up Strategy doesn't produce millions from thin air, like the consolidation method does. But, it does allow you to grow exponentially, quickly. And the beautiful thing about that is, most conventional business loans are 7 year loans. So let's say you performed 4 acquisitions, two $5 million dollar companies, one $10 million, one $20 million, and one $40 million dollar company. And you stopped and never bought another company.

That is $80 million dollars in business loans that are being paid down every day, by the businesses themselves!

So...let's say you don't even grow them at all.

In 7 years, those business loans will be completely paid off and you will own a portfolio worth $80 million!

Talk about a paradigm shift in business!

So there you have it. Our two core acquisition strategies: Consolidation or "Roll Up" and the "Ladder Up" Acquisition Strategy.

Either one will make you millions. Our smartest partners employ both!

Why this works:

- Larger businesses are easier to systematize (they already have infrastructure)
- You gain credibility faster (you're not just a small business owner anymore)
- You can attract better talent and management
- Your exit options improve dramatically

The downside? Larger businesses cost more upfront. You need more capital, more sophisticated financing, and more operational expertise. But... you are buying a business with all of that in place, and for experienced acquirers who have done a few deals, laddering up is often the fastest path to a massive exit.

STRATEGY #3: THE VIRTUAL ROLL-UP

This is cutting-edge territory. Not everyone is ready for this, but we want to plant the seed because it represents the future of consolidation strategies.

A **virtual roll-up** is when you pool together multiple business owners in the same industry—without actually owning their businesses—with a shared agreement to sell the entire portfolio to private equity in 5 years.

How it works:

Instead of you personally buying 10 medical spas, you become the organizer. You bring together 20-50 med spa owners across the United States who agree to:

1. Participate in a pooled entity structure
2. Implement common systems and branding
3. Share best practices and resources
4. Sell together as one large enterprise in 5 years

Why would they agree to this?

Because individually, each med spa might sell for a 5X multiple. But pooled together as a $150-300 million revenue enterprise, they can command a 10-15X multiple.

The math is staggering:

- Individual sale: $5 million business × 5X multiple = $25 million to owner
- Pooled sale: $5 million business × 12X multiple = $60 million to

owners

The owner more than doubles their exit proceeds just by participating in the virtual roll-up.

And you, as the organizer, take a percentage for structuring the deal, providing systems, and managing the consolidation.

This model is being used right now in med spas, dental practices, insurance agencies, and other fragmented professional services.

It's not theory. It's happening.

And it represents a massive opportunity for sophisticated entrepreneurs who understand consolidation thesis and can organize business owners around a common goal.

WHICH STRATEGY SHOULD YOU CHOOSE?

Here's our honest advice:

If you're just starting out:

- Buy a platform company ($3-5M revenue)
- Do 2-3 tuck-in acquisitions in the first 3 years
- Focus on one industry
- Build systems (use Chapter 12)
- Aim for a $20-40M exit in 7-10 years

If you already own a business:

- Build systems (use Chapter 12)

- Acquire complementary bolt-on businesses
- Install marketing and sales systems
- Do tuck-ins to consolidate your market
- Aim for a $15-30M exit in 5-7 years

If you're sophisticated and well-capitalized:

- Consider the ladder-up strategy
- Or organize a virtual roll-up in a fragmented industry
- Aim for a $50-100M+ exit in 5-10 years

The key is to choose a strategy and commit to it.

Don't buy random businesses. Don't chase shiny objects. Don't mix strategies halfway through.

Pick your thesis. Build your empire. Execute relentlessly.

THE CRITICAL MISTAKE PEOPLE MAKE

We've seen hundreds of acquisition deals.

And we can tell you the biggest mistake people make is:

They acquire a bunch of small businesses that require a ton of work to manage. Clearly there is no exit strategy.

They buy a business because it looks like a good deal. Then another one. Then another one. Five years later, they own a random collection of small businesses with no coherent strategy and no obvious buyer.

That's not an empire. That's a portfolio of random assets.

Diversified, yes. And if that's your goal, great!

Easy to consolidate and 2x your exit multiple? Not at all.

Before you buy your first business, decide:

- Are you building for cash flow or exit?
- If exit, who's your target buyer? (Private equity? Strategic acquirer? Individual buyer?)
- What multiple do you need to hit to make the exit worthwhile?
- How many acquisitions do you need to get there?
- What's your timeline?

Answer those questions FIRST. Then structure every acquisition around that strategy.

That's how you build a $50M, $100M, or $200M empire.

ACTION STEPS

1. **Choose your consolidation thesis.** What industry will you dominate? Make the decision this week.
2. **Identify your platform company.** If you don't have one yet, start searching for a $3-5M revenue business in your target industry.
3. **Create your acquisition pipeline.** Use the sourcing strategies from Chapter 11 to build a list of 50-100 potential tuck-in

acquisitions in your industry.

4. **Build your financial model.** Map out the next 5-7 years: How many acquisitions? What EBITDA growth? What exit multiple?

5. **Assemble your team.** You can't do this alone. You need an M&A advisor, a CPA familiar with business acquisitions, an attorney, and a lender relationship.

6. **Study successful roll-ups.** Research companies in your industry that have successfully exited to private equity. What did they do? How long did it take? What multiple did they achieve?

7. **Take action.** The best time to start building an empire was 5 years ago. The second-best time is today.

CHAPTER 14

EXIT WHEN THE TIME IS RIGHT

You've built your empire. You've acquired multiple businesses. You've implemented systems. You've grown EBITDA year over year.

Now comes the moment that makes or breaks everything: the exit.

This is where generational wealth is created or lost. Where years of work either pay off spectacularly or disappoint. Where a $20 million business sells for $25 million... or $15 million.

The difference? Preparation.

Most business owners think about their exit 12-18 months before they want to sell. That's 24-48 months too late...

The best exits are planned 3-5 years in advance. Every decision you make during those years should be designed to maximize your exit multiple and attract the right buyer.

This chapter is about getting that right.

GET OUT WHILE THE GETTING IS GOOD

Let's look at two stories that taught us one of the most important lessons about exits: timing is everything.

STORY #1: PATRICK'S EXIT

Several years ago, Patrick owned a property management company. The business was doing well—growing at 20-25% year over year. It had strong systems, good clients, and solid cash flow.

Patrick started getting that feeling. You know the one. The sense that maybe it's time to move on to the next thing.

A lot of people in that position would have said, "Why sell now? Things are great. Let's ride this wave as long as possible. Let's squeeze every last dollar out of this business."

Patrick didn't do that.

He got out while the getting was good. He sold the business at a fair price, took his chips off the table, and moved on to the next opportunity.

Here's what happened after he left:

Competitors in the area started realizing how much money they could make from online marketing and SEO. They invested heavily in digital presence. They started dominating the local search results.

The company that bought Patrick's business? They didn't adapt fast enough.

Their growth rate went from 20-25% per year to 5%.

If Patrick had held on for "just one more year" or "just a little more growth," he would have been the one dealing with that collapse in growth. His business would have been worth significantly less. Or worse, he would have been stuck trying to compete in a completely different marketing landscape that he hadn't prepared for.

But because he got out when things were good—not when they were desperate—he was able to capture maximum value and avoid the downturn entirely.

STORY #2: THE CRYPTO LESSON

But let's be honest with you: we've also made the opposite mistake.

With cryptocurrency, Patrick got greedy. He watched his positions grow, and instead of taking profits when things were good, he held on. He kept thinking, "It'll go higher. Just a little more. Just a little longer."

Then the market crashed.

He left massive gains on the table because he didn't get out while the getting was good. He fell victim to FOMO—fear of missing out.

THE PATTERN WE SEE EVERYWHERE

This isn't just Patrick's story. We see this pattern constantly with business owners, real estate investors, and entrepreneurs.

They wait. They wait for more money. They wait for better multiples. They wait for one more good year.

Then something happens. Interest rates shoot up. The market crashes. A recession hits. A competitor disrupts the industry. Regulatory changes wipe out profitability.

And the opportunity they had—the exit they could have taken—evaporates.

Here's what we've learned:

When things are good, when markets are strong, when your business is performing well, when you have a positive forecast and a history of growth—that might be exactly the right time to exit.

Not because things are bad. But because things are good.

The best exits happen when you don't desperately need to sell. When you have options. When buyers are competing for your business because it's performing exceptionally.

The worst exits happen when you're forced to sell. When growth has stalled. When you've missed the window.

Don't get greedy.

Don't let fear of missing out keep you from taking a life-changing exit.

If you've built something valuable and someone offers you generational wealth for it, seriously consider taking the deal—even if you think it might be worth more in two years.

Because in two years, it might be worth nothing.

Timing is everything.

We'll show you how to actually determine the right time to exit, how to prepare for maximum value, and how to execute the sale properly.

IDENTIFY YOUR TARGET ACQUIRER FIRST

Before you do anything else, you need to answer one question:

Who's going to buy your business?

Not "someday when I'm ready to sell." Right now. Today.

Because everything you do from this moment forward should be designed to make your business attractive to that specific buyer.

There are four main types of buyers:

1. PRIVATE EQUITY FIRMS

Private equity (PE) firms pool investor capital to acquire businesses, grow them, and sell them for a profit in 3-7 years.

What they want:

- Businesses doing $2-10 million in EBITDA (sweet spot for most PE)
- Predictable, recurring revenue
- Strong management team that can run without the owner
- Clean financials and operations
- Growth potential

What they pay:

- 6-8X EBITDA for mid-market deals
- Sometimes higher for fast-growing or strategic acquisitions

Pros:

- Can handle larger deals
- Experienced buyers who move quickly
- Often have capital ready to deploy

Cons:

- Will demand thorough due diligence
- May replace management
- Cultural fit matters (see below)
- May pay less than a Strategic Buyer

2. STRATEGIC BUYERS

Strategic buyers are larger companies in your industry or adjacent industries who want to acquire your business to expand their offerings, geography, or market share.

What they want:

- Complementary businesses that enhance their portfolio
- Access to new markets or customers
- Intellectual property, patents, or proprietary processes
- Elimination of competition

What they pay:

- Often 8-12X EBITDA or higher
- Will pay premium for unique IP or strategic value
- Sometimes 20-30X for game-changing acquisitions

Pros:

- Highest multiples
- Appreciate unique value propositions
- Often care less about perfect systems (they'll integrate into theirs)

Cons:

- Harder to find the right fit
- Longer sales process
- May want to absorb your business completely

3. FAMILY OFFICES

Family offices are private wealth management firms that invest on behalf of ultra-high-net-worth families.

What they want:

- Cash-flowing businesses with long-term stability
- Lower risk than PE or venture investments
- Businesses that preserve capital and generate income

What they pay:

- 5-8X EBITDA typically
- Sometimes higher for businesses with strong track records

Pros:

- Long-term thinking (not flipping in 3-5 years)
- Less aggressive than PE
- May allow you to stay involved

Cons:

- Each family office has unique criteria
- Decision-making can be slower
- Smaller deal sizes typically

4. INDIVIDUAL BUYERS

Other entrepreneurs, executives, or investors buying businesses individually (often using SBA loans).

What they want:

- Owner-operated businesses they can run themselves
- Businesses under $5M in value (SBA loan limits)
- Simple, understandable business models

What they pay:

- 3-5X EBITDA typically
- Lower multiples than institutional buyers

Pros:

- Easier transaction process
- More personal relationship
- May care about preserving your legacy

Cons:

- Lowest multiples
- Financing can fall through
- Limited to smaller deals

DESIGN YOUR BUSINESS FOR YOUR BUYER

Here's the key insight that changes everything:

Once you know who your target buyer is, you design your entire business to match what they want.

IF YOU'RE TARGETING PRIVATE EQUITY:

- Standardize operations across all locations
- Implement common branding and SOPs
- Build a strong management team that doesn't need you

- Create predictable recurring revenue
- Document everything
- Show consistent EBITDA growth year over year

IF YOU'RE TARGETING STRATEGIC BUYERS:

- Focus on what makes you unique
- Develop proprietary processes or IP
- Build customer relationships that can be transferred
- Demonstrate competitive advantages
- Create synergies with likely acquirers

IF YOU'RE TARGETING FAMILY OFFICES:

- Emphasize stability and cash flow consistency
- Show long-term customer relationships
- Highlight low-risk, predictable operations
- Demonstrate sustainable growth

The worst thing you can do? Build a business without knowing who will buy it. You'll end up with something nobody wants to pay premium multiples for.

Start building relationships with potential acquirers 3-5 years before you want to sell.

Get to know PE firms in your industry. Attend conferences where strategic buyers are present. Have conversations. Ask what they're looking for. Then design your business to be exactly that.

CULTURE MATTERS TODAY

10-15 years ago, PE firms had a reputation for "rape and pillage." They'd buy a company, strip out assets, load it with debt, drive employees into the ground working 70-hour weeks, kill morale, and flip it for a profit.

Culture didn't matter. People didn't matter. Only financials mattered.

Today is different.

Most PE firms we work with are people-first companies. They understand that culture drives performance. They care about employee retention, customer satisfaction, and sustainable growth.

But not all of them.

This is critical: you need to find a buyer that matches your culture.

If you've spent years building a company where people love working, where clients are treated like family, where values matter—don't sell to a buyer who will destroy all of that in year one.

Do your due diligence on the buyer just like they do due diligence on you.

Ask:

- How do they treat employees at acquired companies?
- What happens to management teams post-acquisition?
- What's their reputation in the industry?

- Can you talk to owners of businesses they've previously acquired?

This matters for two reasons:

First, you likely care about the people you've worked with for years. Selling to someone who will treat them poorly feels terrible.

Second, if the buyer destroys culture and performance tanks, your earn-out or seller financing could be at risk. If the business fails post-acquisition, you might not get fully paid.

Culture is not soft. It's financial.

THE 11 VALUE DRIVERS

Patrick is a Certified Exit Planning Advisor (CEPA). He's helped hundreds of business owners prepare for and execute successful exits.

There are 11 key factors that determine your business value and the multiple you'll receive. Any one of these being weak will tank your valuation.

Let's go through all of them.

1. FINANCIAL PERFORMANCE

You might have heard this before, but it warrants repeating: Cash flow is king.

Buyers are buying future cash flow. If your EBITDA is inconsistent, declining, or uncertain, your multiple drops dramatically.

Key questions:

- Are your net profits over 20%? (industry dependent)

- Do you have a history of growth, or is it up and down?
- Is your bookkeeping clean, organized, and following GAAP standards?
- Can a buyer trust your financials, or will they find surprises in due diligence?

What to do:

- Clean up your books 2-3 years before exit
- Show consistent EBITDA growth (even 10-15% annually is great)
- Eliminate owner discretionary expenses that inflate your lifestyle but hurt EBITDA
- Hire a professional CFO or controller if you don't have one

2. INDUSTRY OUTLOOK

Is your industry growing or dying?

If you're in newspaper publishing or retail video rental, your business is worth less no matter how well it performs. Buyers discount declining industries heavily.

If you're in healthcare services, technology, or other growing sectors, you get a premium.

You can't change your industry, but you can:

- Pivot to growth areas within your industry
- Diversify revenue streams to reduce industry risk

- Position yourself as the company thriving despite industry challenges

3. OWNER DEPENDENCE

This is probably the biggest value killer.

If the business can't run without you, buyers see massive risk. They're not buying a business—they're buying a job that requires your specific talents.

And that's worth much less.

Key questions:

- Does the business rely on you for day-to-day operations?
- Do clients expect to work with you personally?
- Are key relationships dependent on your presence?
- Do you have documented processes, or is everything in your head?

What to do:

- Implement Robert's automation systems from Chapter 12 (PDPs, MIOs, Scoreboards, DGRAC roles)
- Remove yourself from operations 12-24 months before exit
- Build a management team that can run the business without you
- Document everything

Think about the wheel analogy from Chapter 13. Is the owner the hub, or are systems and processes the hub?

If you're the hub, your business is worth 30-50% less than it should be.

4. UNIQUE VALUE PROPOSITION

How differentiated are you from competitors?

Here's the test: If we see your marketing and your competitor's marketing, and we remove both logos, can anybody tell the difference?

If not, you have no differentiation. You're a commodity. And commodities get commodity prices and commodity multiples. The business is likely heavily dependent on relationships. And when that is the case, a change in staff can mean the loss of a lot of business.

Additionally, if you don't have a solid USP, you aren't able to charge enough in the market and your margins are probably suffering.

Key questions:

- What do you do that nobody else does?
- Why do customers choose you over competitors?
- What would customers lose if you went out of business?

Common differentiation areas:

- Quality of service
- Quality of product
- Customer experience
- Proprietary processes or technology
- Unique positioning or category creation

What to do:

- Develop and articulate a clear unique value proposition
- Raise prices to match your new USP, this raises your valuation
- Build it into all marketing and sales materials
- Make sure customers know why you're different
- Document any proprietary processes or IP

5. FUTURE GROWTH POTENTIAL

Buyers pay for future earnings, not past earnings.

If your market is saturated and you have 80% market share with no room to grow, you're worth less than a company with 5% market share and massive growth potential.

Key questions:

- What's your total addressable market (TAM)?
- What percentage of that market do you currently own?
- What's your growth trajectory?
- Are there untapped markets, products, or services you could expand into?

What to do:

- Demonstrate realistic growth opportunities
- Show plans for geographic expansion, new products, or adjacent

markets

- Prove you haven't maxed out your potential

6. CUSTOMER CONCENTRATION RISK

If one customer represents more than 15% of your revenue, you're at risk.

Buyers will discount your valuation significantly because if that customer leaves post-acquisition, the business tanks.

What to do:

- Diversify your customer base 2-3 years before exit
- No single customer should exceed 15% of gross revenue
- If you have large customers, get long-term contracts in place

7. VENDOR DEPENDENCE

Same principle applies to vendors.

If you're dependent on one key supplier and they go away, your business is at risk.

What to do:

- Have multiple vendor options for critical supplies
- Document relationships with backup suppliers
- Show you're not vulnerable to supply chain disruption

8. MARKETING DIVERSIFICATION

Don't rely on one marketing channel.

If 100% of your leads come from Facebook ads, what happens when Facebook changes the algorithm?

What to do:

- Have at least 3 "light switches" for lead generation
- Examples: Facebook ads, Google ads, email marketing, SEO, referrals, direct mail
- Show that if one channel fails, you have others

9. NET PROMOTER SCORE (NPS)

This is what professional buyers look at to measure customer satisfaction.

NPS is simple. You ask customers one question: "On a scale of 0-10, how likely are you to recommend our business to friends or family?"

- Promoters (9-10): Loyal enthusiasts who will refer others
- Passives (7-8): Satisfied but unenthusiastic customers
- Detractors (0-6): Unhappy customers who can damage your brand

NPS Score = % Promoters - % Detractors.

World-class NPS is 50+. Good is 30-50. Anything below 30 is a red flag.

What to do:

- Implement NPS surveys 2-3 years before exit
- Track the score over time
- Fix issues that create detractors
- Maximize your Google reviews, social media presence, and online reputation

10. RECURRING REVENUE

This is one of the most powerful value drivers.

Buyers love predictable, recurring revenue because it reduces risk and increases future cash flow certainty.

Examples:

- Property management: sign owner once, manage property forever (theoretically).
- SaaS subscriptions: monthly or annual recurring revenue
- Membership programs: ongoing monthly payments
- Service contracts: annual maintenance agreements

What to do:

- Create recurring revenue models in your business 2-3 years before exit
- For service businesses: develop tiered membership programs (Platinum, Gold, Silver)

- For product businesses: create subscription or replenishment models
- Target recurring revenue to cover your fixed operating costs

A plumbing company with $400K/month in recurring revenue from maintenance contracts is worth significantly more than one that relies entirely on new customer acquisition.

A plumbing company that is 100% recurring revenue might demand over twice the value of a counterpart plumbing company with same EBITDA. You should maximize your company's ability to produce recurring revenue at all times, but especially prior to an exit.

11. COMPANY CULTURE, TEAM STRENGTH

Strong teams drive strong performance.

Buyers want businesses where employees are engaged, motivated, and committed to delivering results.

What to do:

- Measure employee engagement annually (Gallup has the best research on this)
- Implement retention programs for key employees
- Document your culture and values
- Show low turnover and high employee satisfaction
- Measure Net Promoter Score annually

Buyers will pay more for a business where the team will stay post-acquisition than one where half the team leaves the moment you sell.

THE 2-3 YEAR EXIT PREPARATION TIMELINE

The absolute best time to start preparing for your exit is 3-5 years before you want to sell.

Here's what that timeline looks like:

YEARS 5 - 4 BEFORE EXIT:

Financial house:

- Clean up your financials
- Implement proper accounting systems (GAAP compliant)
- Remove owner discretionary expenses
- Show consistent EBITDA growth

Operations:

- Implement systems from Chapter 12
- Remove yourself from day-to-day operations
- Build management team
- Document all processes

Growth:

- Maximize recurring revenue
- Diversify customer base (no client over 15% of revenue)

- Expand marketing channels
- Show growth trajectory

YEARS 3 - 2 BEFORE EXIT:

Value drivers:

- Implement NPS tracking
- Build unique value proposition
- Create customer retention programs
- Strengthen team and culture

Buyer relationships:

- Start conversations with potential acquirers
- Understand exactly what they want
- Adjust business to match buyer criteria
- Get business valued by professionals

YEAR OF EXIT:

Pre-sale:

- Hire an M&A advisor (like Elkridge)
- Get formal business valuation
- Prepare due diligence materials

- Organize all documentation

Sale process:

- Market to qualified buyers
- Field offers
- Negotiate LOI (Letter of Intent)
- Complete due diligence
- Close transaction

If you're considering an exit and would like assistance with any part of the Exit Preparation Process, reach out to our team using the email in the Resources section at the end of this book, and we'll get back to you swiftly.

EXIT PLANNING EXPERTISE

The **Certified Exit Planning Advisor (CEPA)** is one of the most rigorous certifications in business exit and succession planning.

The CEPA program covers everything from business valuation and tax optimization to deal structuring and value acceleration strategies. It requires extensive training in exactly what we're about to discuss: how to prepare a business for sale and execute an exit at maximum value.

PRIVATE EQUITY VS. STRATEGIC BUYERS

The short answer: it depends on what you've built and what you want.

Choose Private Equity if:

- You've built a standardized, scalable business

- You want a straightforward transaction
- You're targeting 6-8X EBITDA multiples
- You don't mind the business changing post-sale
- You want a second bite of the apple. Many times, you stay on as a minority owner and continue to run the business with their assistance and resources for scaling.

Choose Strategic Buyers if:

- You have unique IP, processes, or positioning
- You want the highest possible multiple (8-15X+)
- You're willing to wait for the right buyer
- Synergy with the buyer creates exceptional value

Consider Both:

Here's our recommendation: **explore both private equity and strategic buyers.**

Don't limit yourself to one path. Different buyers will value your business differently based on what they see.

A PE firm might offer 7X. A strategic buyer who can integrate your business into their platform might offer 10X.

Cast a wide net. Let the market tell you what your business is worth.

BIGGEST MISTAKES BUSINESS OWNERS MAKE

After years of helping clients with exits, here are the mistakes we see over and over:

1. Waiting until they're ready to retire to think about exit

By then it's too late to maximize value. You need 2-3 years minimum.

2. Not knowing who their buyer is

You can't design a business for maximum value if you don't know who's buying it.

3. Being too dependent on the owner

This kills 30-50% of your value instantly.

4. Having inconsistent financial performance

Buyers heavily discount volatile EBITDA. They want predictability.

5. Not getting professional help

Selling a business is not DIY. You need an M&A advisor, experienced attorney, and professional valuation.

6. Accepting the first offer without shopping the deal

Always get multiple offers. Competition drives prices up.

7. Poor due diligence preparation

If you don't have documents organized, buyers will walk away or dramatically lower their offers.

8. Not minimizing tax write offs at least 2 years ahead

Lenders loan on what is on tax reports, not your P&L. Get them to be in alignment at least 2 years ahead of selling.

Don't make these mistakes. They cost millions.

WHEN IS THE RIGHT TIME TO EXIT?

This chapter is called "Exit When The Time Is Right"—but when is that exactly?

The honest answer: when you've maximized enterprise value and found the right buyer.

Not when you're burned out. Not when you're bored. Not when you're 65 because that's retirement age.

The right time to exit is when:

1. You've achieved your financial goals
2. The business is operating at peak value
3. You have multiple interested buyers
4. The market conditions are favorable
5. Your personal readiness aligns with business readiness

For many entrepreneurs following the consolidation thesis from Chapter 13, that's 5-10 years after your first acquisition.

You've rolled up 5-10 businesses. You've grown EBITDA to $3-5 million or more. You're getting 7-10X multiples. You're walking away with $20-50 million.

That's when you exit.

Not a moment before you're ready. Not a moment after peak value.

Timing is everything.

ACTION STEPS

1. **Identify your target acquirer today.** Research PE firms, strategic buyers, and family offices in your industry. Who's most likely to buy your business in 5 years?

2. **Get a professional valuation.** You need to know what your business is worth today and what it could be worth with improvements.

3. **Create your 3-year exit plan.** Map out the improvements you need to make year by year to maximize value.

4. **Remove yourself from operations.** Start the process today. Your business should run without you.

5. **Start building buyer relationships.** Attend industry conferences. Connect with PE firms. Have exploratory conversations about what they're looking for.

6. **Hire professional help.** Work with an M&A advisor to prepare for and execute your exit. The ROI is 10-100X what you pay in fees.

7. **Document everything.** Start organizing all contracts, financials, customer lists, employee files, and operational procedures. Buyers will want to see all of it.

CHAPTER 15

LEAN INTO IT

You've made it to the penultimate chapter.

You've learned how to build your financial foundation, how to acquire businesses, how to automate operations, how to create empires and exit at maximum value.

Now let's talk about something that ties everything together. Something that separates people who are spectacularly successful from people who just go through the motions.

It's not another strategy. It's not another framework. Nor another tool.

It's a philosophy about how to live our lives.

And it starts with a conversation Robert's been having with people for about 15 years. The exact structure of the discussion of course differs, but the basic message or question is the same:

"Robert, don't you have a hobby?"

His answer always surprises.

Here's why.

THE HOBBY MYTH

People who "need" hobbies are typically people who don't like their job.

Of course these are some, very few exceptions, but in general that's the truth nobody wants to say out loud.

They don't like their job. Or they don't like their life. Or they don't like their marriage. Or they don't like something fundamental about how they spend their days.

And they need an escape. The hobby becomes their escape. The thing that makes the rest of it bearable.

Fishing. Golf. Collecting things. Watching sports. Binge-watching TV series. Video games. Whatever it is.

They need that escape because the other 40, 50, 60 hours a week are draining their life energy doing something they don't want to do.

Here's what Robert believes instead:

Build a life you enjoy with people you like spending time with, and you'll never feel you need a hobby outside of what you're doing day-to-day or week-to-week.

If you love what you do, you don't need an escape from it.

Now, let's be clear: going to the gym isn't a hobby. You do that for your health. Playing tennis with his wife Diana isn't a hobby—it's spending time with someone he loves while staying active.

A hobby is something you do to escape. To distract yourself from the life you don't really want to be living.

If you're doing something because it adds value to your life—because you genuinely enjoy it, because it aligns with who you are—then it's not a hobby. It's *part of the design* of how you want to live.

But you don't need to add more things to your life. You don't need another distraction. You don't need another escape.

You'll find more fulfillment in either learning to enjoy what you're already doing, or do something else.

IF YOU LOVE IT, DO IT

Here's the permission we want to give you, because almost no one else will:

If you love working and you love building wealth, just do it.

If you love it, lean into it. Do it for 12 hours a day if that's what brings you joy. Don't apologize for it. Don't feel guilty about it. Don't let anyone tell you that you "should" have balance or "should" have hobbies.

People like Alex Hormozi and GaryVee talk about this extensively. Just be aligned with who you actually are and do that. If you can do that for 12 hours a day and be happy, do it.

And if someone judges you for it? They might not be good friends. Or you might need to set some very firm expectations within that relationship.

Here are some examples:

Fernando, the person who helped us edit this book, loves reading. He loves books. He loves editing. That's why this book came out as good as it did. Fernando loves this work. No one needs to tell him to do it. We paid for his service, obviously. But he loves doing it. He doesn't need an escape or a hobby different from this. He loves this.

Patrick loves speaking to people and getting to understand them. He genuinely gets a high every time we make our partners money. Patrick loves this work.

Robert loves building systems. He loves being an engineer. He loves being an architect. That's what he does for our businesses all the time.

If either of us would not be paid, we would probably somehow still do these things to some extent, even without pay. And that's how you know you've chosen well.

That's how you know you're aligned with who you actually are.

THE JUDGMENT OF OTHERS

Let's address something uncomfortable.

When you commit fully to building wealth, to working 10-12 hours a day, to prioritizing your business and your financial goals—some people will judge you for it.

They'll tell you that you're "too focused on money." That you're "missing out on life." That you "should have balance." That you "need to relax more."

Here's what you need to understand: Those people have a negative mindset that's keeping them behind.

More importantly, they are judging you and clawing you back, keeping you from your potential, because they do that to themselves on a daily basis.

This has nothing to do with you. And this is very important to underline.

If you have people in your life who judge you for being career-focused or money-focused, you should not be in that relationship. Or you should limit that relationship as much as you can.

Now, if they disagree with your choices but don't judge you for them? That's different. Just don't talk business or money with them. Talk about dogs, or hiking, or music, or writing—whatever you have in common. But not money.

Robert talks to writers and artists all the time because he's a creative person and he loves the creative side of things. But he doesn't talk to them about money because they have a very negative mindset around money.

They're the "struggling artist." The "misunderstood" person. The romantic who believes that being broke is somehow noble or authentic.

When in reality, they don't understand how the world works and how money flows. But they don't want to understand. They have the struggling artist mindset, and they're committed to it.

That's fine for them. But it's not fine for you to absorb their judgments and let them slow you down.

If someone believes that more money is a bad thing, you should not be talking to them about money.

It's that simple.

YOU DON'T NEED PERMISSION

Here's what we want you to take away from this final chapter:

You don't need permission to go all-in on building wealth.

You don't need permission to work 12 hours a day if that's what brings you joy.

You don't need permission to prioritize your business over socializing with friends who don't add value to your life.

You don't need permission to cut out distractions, eliminate hobbies that don't serve you, and focus exclusively on the 3-5 things that actually matter to you.

And you definitely don't need permission to ignore the judgment of people who don't understand your drive.

If you love building businesses, build businesses.

If you love creating wealth, create wealth.

If you love the game of acquisition and automation and exits—play that game fully.

Lean into it. Don't apologize for it. Don't water it down. Don't pretend you're "balanced" when you're all-in.

Be who you actually are. Do what you actually love. Focus on what actually matters to you.

Everything else is noise.

THE PATH YOU'VE TRAVELED

Let's take a moment to reflect on what you've learned in this book.

In **Part One**, you built your financial foundation by learning how to:

- Keep track of your finances and net worth properly
- Choose the career path that will bring you most wealth
- Understand and work better with other people

- Make progress quicker by modeling the masters
- Overcome any roadblocks faster with How Sessions
- Prioritize everything and get more done each day
- Managed your life energy and focus
- Keep strengthening your network
- Lived by the #1 principle of success
- Safely and swiftly pass $300,000 in assets

In **Part Two**, you turned assets into passive income through:

- World-class acquisition strategies, and
- Automate businesses so they run without you

In **Part Three**, you learned to create generational wealth by:

- Building empires through consolidation
- Knowing exactly when and how to exit for maximum value
- Leaning into who you actually are

It's not a get-rich-quick scheme. It's not a shortcut. It's not a hack.

It's a systematic, repeatable process for doubling your net worth and passive income year after year.

Thousands of people have done it before you. Thousands more will do it after you.

The question is: Will you be one of them?

SOME FINAL WORDS FROM BOTH OF US

Firstly, if you've made it this far, you're not a casual reader. You're serious about building wealth. You're serious about financial freedom. You're serious about creating something bigger than yourself.

That's exactly who we wrote this book for.

Everything in these pages works. We know it works because we've tested all of it ourselves. And we've helped dozens of clients do it. We've seen the results, over and over again.

But here's the thing: information without action is worthless.

You can know everything in this book and, by this time next year, still end up exactly where you are today... if you don't take action.

So here's our challenge to you:

Pick one thing from this book. Just one. And implement it this week.

Not next month. Not after you "get ready." This week.

Start your How Sessions. Update your balance sheet. Reach out to one business broker. Do the Warren Buffett 25/5 exercise. Document one process in your business.

Just one thing. Then build from there.

That's how empires are built. One action at a time. One decision at a time.

Second, throughout this book, we've talked about strategies and frameworks and tools. We've given you the roadmap to financial freedom.

But the real secret—the thing that separates people who succeed from people who don't—is this:

Love the process.

If you only love the destination (the money, the exit, the freedom), you'll burn out before you get there. The journey is too long. The work is too hard. The setbacks are too frequent.

But if you can learn to love the process itself—the acquisitions, the negotiations, the systems-building, the problem-solving, the growth—then you'll never want to stop.

And if you never want to stop, you can't fail. You'll just keep going until you succeed.

So find the parts of this process that light you up. The parts that make you excited to wake up at 4 AM and work. The parts that don't feel like work at all.

Then lean into those parts. Build your life around them. Make them your priorities.

That's when wealth stops being a goal and becomes a byproduct of doing what you love.

That's Elkridge Path.

ACTION STEPS

1. **If you haven't already, pick one chapter from this book to implement its lessons this week.** Just one. Read it again. Take the action steps. Actually do them.

CHAPTER 16

THE FULL CIRCLE OF WEALTH

When you've automated your income, built your empire, and created generational wealth, the natural next question is: *Now what?*

The answer... is to give back.

Not because it looks good on social media or because someone told you philanthropy is good business. You give back because abundance without contribution leaves you empty. The true reward of mastering business and life is the ability—and responsibility—to uplift others.

During our *Automate* conversation, we discussed how automation is about more than systems. It's about creating capacity—capacity for peace, for family, and for giving. Once you've freed your time and stabilized your finances, you finally have the bandwidth to focus outward.

That's the full circle of wealth. You start by learning to earn. Then you master keeping and multiplying what you earn. And finally, you learn to *return*—to reinvest part of what you've built back into others.

WHY WE GIVE

Giving isn't about guilt or obligation. It's about alignment.

Patrick often says, "We're big believers in sharing the wealth we attain with others—not because it's good PR, but because it's the right thing to do."

The Bible calls this *stewardship.* Other traditions call it *karma.* Whatever your worldview, the idea is the same: when you're blessed, you bless others.

"The best way for humanity to help the poor is by not becoming or staying poor themselves."

That statement shocks some people, but it's true. You can't help the sick if you're bedridden. You can't help the poor if you're broke. And you can't mentor future entrepreneurs if you're still in survival mode.

Creating abundance in your own life is what *enables* you to give back—sustainably, intelligently, and with real impact.

HOW TO GIVE BACK INTENTIONALLY

In the *Automate* session, we spoke about creating self-managing teams and self-sustaining businesses, so you're no longer the bottleneck. That freedom allows you to direct your energy into higher-level purposes.

Here's how to make giving part of that same intentional design:

1. **Start Local.** The greatest opportunities to serve are often within reach—mentoring at a local business incubator, sponsoring scholarships, or teaching basic financial literacy at your church or community center.

2. **Focus on Education.** Access to education—especially for children—is the highest-leverage way to change lives. A single scholarship or after-school program can compound its impact for decades.

3. **Give Skills, Not Just Money.** The entrepreneurs we mentor

through Elkridge Advisors often realize their knowledge is more valuable than a check. Teaching someone how to run their books, structure deals, or communicate value can change their trajectory forever.

4. **Build "Automated Generosity."** Just like you automate savings or investments, automate giving. Set up recurring donations, endowments, or profit-sharing contributions to causes you care about. Make generosity systematic so it scales as your wealth grows.

5. **Involve Your Team and Family.** Let your children and employees see your giving in action. Invite them to choose causes or volunteer alongside you. It builds culture, unity, and gratitude.

"Money doesn't change who you are—it reveals who you are."

If greed or fear dominate your decisions, wealth will only magnify that. If gratitude and love guide you, wealth amplifies your ability to do good.

Patrick believes giving is how you prove to yourself that money doesn't own you anymore.

When you can part with a portion joyfully, you know you're free.

He also reminds clients that philanthropy is not just charity—it can be a strategic way to magnify your life's purpose. Supporting education, entrepreneurship, or environmental restoration are all forms of legacy creation. They can align beautifully with your values and your mission.

YOUR GIFT TO OTHERS

In 2015, Robert led a pro bono training for 22 nonprofit directors in Mexico. When he asked, "How can people best help the poor"', everyone listed things like better education or more subsidies.

Robert said, "No. The best way to help the poor is by not becoming or staying poor yourself."

If all of us learned to take care of ourselves well, we'd be far more capable of helping others. As such, the best gift you can ever give is to become an example of abundance, wisdom, and love.

That's part of what giving back really means. It's not just about writing checks—it's about becoming the kind of person whose life inspires others to rise.

ACTION STEPS

Reflect on your journey through this book. Ask yourself:

- *Who can I empower with what I've learned?*
- *What cause, person, or community needs what I now have in surplus—knowledge, time, or capital?*
- *How can I make giving an intentional, recurring part of my wealth system?*

Then, take one small, specific step this week: sponsor a student, donate to a local nonprofit, volunteer, plant trees, or teach someone something you've mastered. That's how legacy begins.

CLOSING THOUGHT

Elkridge Path is more than just about doubling your net worth. It's about doubling your *impact.*

When you give back, you close the loop between success and significance. You prove that wealth, at its highest level, isn't about accumulation—it's about contribution.

Resources

ELKRIDGE ADVISORS WEALTH ACCELERATION SERVICES

If you already own a profitable company or asset portfolio and would like our team to help you with items such as:

- Business Preparation & Presentation Services
- Direct Outreach To Buyers, Investors, or Sellers
- SBA or Other Loan Application Assistance
- Financial, Legal, or Operational Due Diligence
- Financial Assistance Services, Such As Tax Efficiency
- And Much More

Just email our team at office@elkridgeadvisors.com, letting us know what you'd like help with, and we'll get back to you swiftly.

ACCESS TO ALL TOOLS & TEMPLATES

If you'd like access to any of the templates and tools mentioned across the book, such as:

- Editable Profit & Loss Statements or Balance Sheets
- Journaling Tools With Built-In Wealth Acceleration Prompts
- Suggested Playlists for Meditation or Focused Work
- Business Tools Such As Scoreboards, PDPs, and JDs
- Community Forums For Networking & Q&A (We also answer)
- Our Most Up-To-Date Tax Efficiency Strategies
- Our Most Up-To-Date Investment Recommendations
- And Much More

Just sign up at:

www.elkridgeadvisors.com/resources

www.ingramcontent.com/pod-product-compliance
Lightning Source LLC
LaVergne TN
LVHW090311210926
848480LV00001B/212